LIFE'S
STORMS

To my dear husband, Gary, who patiently suffers
through my endless projects.
Thank you dear for all of your help and support.
I love you!

*"You shall love the Lord your God with all your heart
and with all your soul and with all your strength
and with all your mind, and your neighbor as yourself."*
Luke 10:27 ESV

LIFE'S STORMS

CLARE HULSEMAN MCCULLAH

XULON PRESS

Xulon Press
2301 Lucien Way #415
Maitland, FL 32751
407.339.4217
www.xulonpress.com

Paperback ISBN-13: 978-1-6628-4750-9
eBook ISBN-13: 978-1-6628-4751-6

Table of Contents

Chapter 1
Officer Chad Brown

Mid-April 1977

Sargent Chad Brown of the Nebraska Highway Patrol set quietly in his office in Chadron listening to KLRC, the local radio station. He consumed his last sip of coffee before he went back out into the cold. He noticed the temperatures were falling. There wasn't a doubt in his mind that snow was on its way. A word he almost hated. People often did stupid things in the snow to the point of jeopardizing their own lives and the lives of others just to get from point A to point B. He shook his head, grabbed his hat and gloves, and left the warm confines of his office. He was headed south on Highway 385 toward Alliance. No one had to tell him that it would be a long night.

His territory covered from the Wyoming border on the west to the South Dakota border on the north. The City of Alliance was the southern point of his territory with the Sand Hills in between Chadron and Alliance. With the assistance of his captain and eleven other troopers, they covered a total of eighty square miles. With the snow coming, the size of the territory was growing by leaps and bounds.

As Officer Brown turned onto Highway 385, he took mental inventory of the contents of his 1976 Ford LTD. He was satisfied the vehicle had been properly equipped and maintained. The maintenance shop added studded tires to improve his traction. Tire chains were kept in the trunk just in case they were needed when the studded tires weren't quite enough. This car was heavy enough with the trunk loaded, it would get the officer almost anywhere he needed to go. It just never hurt to be cautious when you are responsible for the citizens in the State of Nebraska.

A light dusting of snow was beginning to fall as Chad arrived near the gates of Chadron State Park. He hoped the snow wouldn't be too deep until later in the day. He needed to get to Alliance before noon. There was nothing to block the snow from the intense winds of the prairie. The Table, as the locals called it, was a plateau of very rich farmland about fifteen miles south of Chadron. The snows could blow for miles in the openness. Its residents are descendants of German Immigrates who have worked very hard to preserve a way of life that is dwindling as more and more young people move into the cities for other types of work. Some of the old ways are gone, but others remained. Chad knew he could count on the assistance of the landowners in any emergency. These people had survived the harsh elements for years by working together. It was a way of life for them born out of necessity.

The trip to Alliance was uneventful for the most part. The officer stopped one vehicle for speeding. The driver was going seventy miles per hour in a fifty five mile an hour zone. The Nebraska Legislature reduced the speed limits from seventy to fifty five on the major highways in Nebraska. The reduction in speed limits reduced the amounts of accidents in the heavily popu-lated areas around Lincoln and Omaha but did nothing for the people of Western Nebraska who drive miles and miles with no other cars in sight. Case in point, it is a sixty mile stretch between Chadron and Alliance with only a handful of farmhouses and the small town of Hemingford. You rarely pass another car.

The out of state car contained a driver in his forties by his date of birth on his driver's license. A very young girl holding a sleeping baby, and a teenage boy occupied the backseat. The driver seemed a little upset that he had been stopped. The girl and the boy wouldn't look Officer Brown in the eye. Their behavior wasn't uncommon for people stopped for traffic violations. The public was gen-erally a little afraid of a patrolman. Officer Brown had experienced that kind of fear many, many times. If they didn't show a little fear and respect, then an experienced officer would begin to wonder. Usually, a smile and some polite words eased the tensions. Using the same procedure with this driver seemed to work. The driver relaxed when Sargent Brown issued only a warning ticket to slow him down, then they both went about their day.

By the time Sargent Brown left the Alliance office with the materials in hand that were needed in the Chadron office, it was getting increasingly cloudy, the temperatures were falling, and the snow was starting to fall even faster. There had to be a better way to get paperwork back and forth between the two offices sixty miles apart, Chad thought. He got back into his patrol car to drive back to Chadron. Maybe they will invent a machine for that! As he traveled around the Hemingford exit, he realized the snow getting more intense. The winds had increased in speed with nearly whiteout conditions in some areas. The storm was getting more dramatic as he traveled northward. Chad radioed his captain in the Chadron office to get a report on the weather conditions.

"Jacobson, here," Captain Kyle Jacobson responded to the radio in the same manner every time. One thing is for sure, he's consistent, Chad Brown thought with a smile on his face. The officer had filled his coffee cup and thermos in the Alliance office before he left. He reached over to get another sip of coffee from his half full coffee mug. He still had a full thermos of coffee to stave off the cold. Chad realized he would need every drop if he got stuck in this white mess.

Brown placed his coffee mug back into its holder. He carefully maneuvered the highway as he reached for the radio microphone. "Sargent Brown, Sir. What is the weather like up there?"

"Gee, I'm not sure. I haven't looked outside for an hour or so. Let me check," replied Captain Jacobson. A moment later Jacobson returns to the radio. "I can't hardly see across the highway. Traffic on 385 is moving very slowly. The roads are becoming snow packed and slick up here. Where are you, Brown?"

"I just past the Hemingford turn off and I'm headed your direction. By the way, I have the paperwork you wanted from the Alliance office. I'll bring it to you as soon as I can. Are we going to have to block the highway from Chadron to Alliance tonight? It sure looks like it on this end. The snow is covering the roads, the temperatures are dropping, and the winds are whipping against the car. I sure would hate to have someone caught in this storm and freeze to death."

"So, would I. The publicity would eat us up. I'll call Alliance and shut down the highway leaving there. Then I'll close the highway south out of Chadron. I know there will be people between Alliance and Chadron that make it through our roadblocks. We will have to account for them. Let's get some farmers to help house those stranded motorists along the way. I will call Mr. and Mrs. Mills. They are the last house south of Chadron just up on the Table. Hopefully, we can catch people there. Let's keep motorists from going onto the open roads of the Sandhills where the winds and snow are the most dangerous. I will give you a call after I talk to

Mr. and Mrs. Mills. They are good people. I'm sure they will be willing to help anyone who is stranded." Captain Jacobson stated. He was all business now. Suddenly, he had a plan in place and a mission to carry out. The captain lifted the telephone receiver off of its cradle. He dialed the rotary telephone with one hand and holding the telephone receiver with the other. His eyes glued to a rolodex with the telephone number for Jay Mills.

After talking with Mrs. Mills, Kyle radioed Sargent Brown. "We are all set. You can direct people to the Mills' farm as you retrieve them from the highway. Mrs. Mills stated they will be ready for their guests. She asked people to bring any blankets or pillows they have in their cars into her house. She wanted to keep everyone warm and fed." That young women will make a fine nurse. She certainly cares for the comforts of others, Jacobson thought. The Mills were a fine young couple and a real credit to the farming community.

"Will do, I'm on my way," replied Chad Brown. "I have a feeling this is going to be a very long night. I will keep you posted from this end." Chad placed the radio microphone back into its holder and took another sip of his coffee. One thing about going to the Alliance office, the secretary makes really good coffee in a thirty gallon coffee pot. She keeps plenty of it available for the officers to fill their thermos before going out on the road.

Chapter 2
Henry Hapfield

⁓

To Henry Hapfield, it was pure luxury to leave the alarm clock unset on a weekday. It had been an exhausting week. His wife, Joan, had gone to Denver to be with her ailing father. His father-in-law, Paul, had had so many of these health crises. Henry just chalked this episode up as one more. From their home in Rapid City, South Dakota, it was a seven hour drive to Denver, Colorado in the best of conditions. A very long drive for someone who was near exhaustion. Joan had flown out of the Rapid City airport two days before. She rented a car in Denver and drove to her father's home in Aurora just on the outskirts of Denver. Henry had too many business meetings to leave Rapid City the same day. He had already missed quite a bit of work recently and couldn't spare one more day.

Paul's health had been declining for a decade. He seemed to need more attention since his wife, Alice, passed away five years ago. Joan felt a desperate need to be with her father every time he got sick. To Henry's way of thinking, Paul just wanted to spend time with Joan. Thinking about it, Henry decided maybe he wasn't being fair to the eighty five year old man. Paul had had continuous heart problems for years. The man was simply wearing out.

Henry realized most of his current problem was jealousy. He wanted his wife home with him. Until the end of May, winter could come on the Plains at any time. He hated having Joan traveling to Denver this time of year. Since he loved her, Henry was concerned for Joan's safety. At least he told himself that to ease his mind. Henry decided he needed to do something more constructive.

A friend at work had mentioned the big horn sheep had been seen near Hill City. One thing about living close to the Black Hills, there was always wildlife to see and photograph. Henry looked outside the living room window. It was cloudy. There was a chill to the air. He would love to go for a ride in the Hills. Unfortunately, he had to be a responsible adult and go into the office in about an hour. He made a few pieces of toast with chokecherry jam and brewed a cup of coffee. His coffee was never a good as Joan's. She would have gotten up early and had it ready for him as he came out of the shower. Come to think of it, she really did spoil him. After thirty five years of marriage and three children, they had become very comfortable together. Henry had to admit, he missed his beloved wife.

As Henry entered the bedroom to find a sweater and slacks suitable for work, he was startled by the sound of the telephone on the kitchen wall. To Henry, the telephone was a necessity and a source of aggravation. He thought maybe there was some crisis at work, although he couldn't imagine what it could be this early in the morning. When he picked up the receiver, he could hear a sobbing voice on the other end of the line. He was needed. Joan didn't have to say more than that. He just knew her. She wasn't given to sudden tears or hysteria. If she was crying, there was good reason.

***

"Henry is that you," she managed to say through her tears. A sudden rush of panic hit her. What if he couldn't get here in time? Joan needed her husband's arm around her. She needed him to tell her everything was going to be alright.

"Yes, dear. What's wrong? How is your dad?" He could guess the answers to his questions, but he has been wrong before.

"Dad is much worse. We had to admit him to the hospital about an hour ago. The doctor's say his heart is failing. He won't recover. He's had too many heart attacks. There's just too much damage. Only thirty percent of his heart is functioning. They have him on oxygen, but he can't seem to breathe. The doctors advised us to call the family. They don't expect him live much longer. I need you, honey." With that statement, Joan broke into a full blown flood of tears. Henry wanted so badly to reach through the telephone just to hold his beautiful wife. Just to make her feel loved and secure. Just to make him feel less guilty about being six hundred and fifty miles away.

"I will try to get a flight as soon as I can. Let me call the airport. I will call you right back." Henry found himself saying. He would just have to miss some more work. He hated to call his boss to request additional time off, but Joan was more important. He wouldn't be able to attend several meetings. Hopefully, his boss could find someone to cover for him for a few days.

"Ok, dear. I'm at Dad's right now. I plan to gather some extra clothing for me, and some things Dad wants in the hospital. I will go back up there after I have a bite to eat. Dad is at Mile High Hospital room 218 in the ICU.

"Can you wait at your Dad's until I call back? I stand a better chance of reaching you there. It shouldn't be no more than about thirty minutes."

"Alright, I won't leave until I hear from you." Joan was relieved he was coming to Denver. She needed him right now. Joan realized she should tell Henry that he's needed more often. She made a mental note to talk to him as soon as she saw him in person.

Joan placed the telephone receiver back into its cradle on her father's giant oak desk. The desk had been made by a family friend when Joan was very young. Her dear mother used to polish and clean it with regularity.

Since her mother passed away, the desk like the rest of the house had falling into disrepair. He just didn't seem care about much of anything anymore. To add to the problem was her father's physical health. He didn't have the energy to do the gardening or home repairs that he used to do. He never was a cook or very good inside the house. Those were always her mother's responsibilities. Although looking back on it now, her mother just wore herself out taking care of her father. He required so much care after each of his heart attacks. She failed to take care of herself because she was so busy taking care of him.

Joan walked up the stairs of the old two story Victorian home. At the top of the stairs she turned right and walked down the long hallway to her father's bedroom. When she was a child, these rooms were filled with love and laughter. Memories filled her. She remembered the days when they used to play on the railing leading downstairs until her sister broke her arm. After that, the game was strictly forbidden. Punishable by a spanking on the offender's bottom.

Joan made her way to her father's closet and opened the double doors. There were dirty clothes everywhere. At least to Joan, they were dirty just for the simple fact that they had been on the floor. There wasn't much still hanging in the closet. She picked up several pieces, placed them in a bundle, and planned to launder them later. She managed to find her father's bathrobe on the back of the bathroom door. It needed cleaning. Too dirty for the hospital in Joan's judgement. She opened his dresser drawers in an effort to locate the pair of flannel pajamas she had given him last Christmas. Dad really preferred to sleep in a t-shirt and underwear. Joan thought he needed pajamas to keep him warm in his recliner when he didn't feel like dressing for the day. She thought the pajamas might be good in the hospital especially when he starts to walk around the ward as he gets stronger.

At that moment the reality of the entire situation hit her. She threw the dirty clothing onto her father's bed and fell on top of them in a moment of tears and self-pity. What would she do without her beloved father? He had always been there to listen to her problems no matter how far from home she went. He encouraged and talked to her in a way that made her feel complete. The only other person who made her feel that way was Henry. Dear Henry, who was willing to come all this way to be with her just because she asked him. She was a very lucky woman. With that thought her tears began to subside. She began to think more logically. For now, she would take some extra socks and pajamas to the hospital for her father just to keep him warm in bed. As he needed other things, she would come home to get them or purchase them. The bathrobe could be laundered later. There was no sense in looking too far ahead at this point.

After gathering anything else she thought she might need for her father or herself, Joan walked across the yard to the old single car garage. She opened the double doors, walked between her father's old Ford and the garage wall, and climbed into the old car. The seats were dusty and grimy. She decided she needed to take the car for a good cleaning when she got a break from the hospital. She wondered how much gas was in the old car. Viewing the dashboard, Joan was pleased to know there was half a tank of gasoline if the gauge was correct. She started the vehicle to make sure it would run. After backing out the garage, she left the car in the driveway where it would be easier to load. Driving Dad's car would sure beat relying on taxis to get around Denver. A cold wind was blowing off of the Rockies as she noticed a layer of snow still blanketing the peaks. It was nice to be home again. She just hated the circumstances.

Joan went back into the house. She still had to wait for Henry's telephone call. Joan realized that for the first time she was feeling hungry. A check of Dad's refrigerator was in order. She doubted there was much food in it, but she needed to check. If Dad was going to be in the hospital for a while, then anything that might spoil would need attention anyway. The results for her exploration were just as she suspected. Spoiled milk, molded bread, and slimy veggies awaited her. This definitely wouldn't work. The kitchen cabinets revealed stale crackers, a can of pork n beans, and a few potato chips that were old enough to vote in the next election. Well, eating here wasn't going to happen. Dad's trash can was stacked to the rim with fast food cartons. Well, I know what Dad has been eating, she thought. Joan decided she would have to make a fast food stop for herself on the way to the hospital after Henry called her back.

To fill her time, she gathered the spoiled and expired food from the refrigerator and cabinets. After placing them into the trash can, she pulled the sides of the trash bag to tie it shut. The can was too full to fit the contents into one bag. She opened cabinet door after cabinet door until she found her query. The woman placed the remaining trash in an empty bag. She decided she might as well gather up the trash in the rest of the house. She dusted and vacuumed. She had to be doing something. Joan couldn't sit still and wait with so much work to be done.

***

Henry laid the telephone in its cradle attached to the wall. He grabbed the telephone book from under the kitchen counter. Looking through the telephone book he soon found the number to the Rapid City Airport to book his flight to Denver. There are only two flights a day out of the Rapid City Airport to Denver. Only one of them was a direct flight without any stops. The other was far less direct with stops in Chadron, Scottsbluff, and Cheyenne. He understood why they called that plane the "Puddle Jumper". He would take that flight if he had to, but it wasn't his preferred choice. Henry called the airport. Both flights to Denver were booked solid. The next available flight was in three more days. Henry decided he could drive to Denver faster than that. He called Joan back. He knew she would wait for his call. Henry expected she would pick up the phone on the first ring. Sure enough the phone barely rang once when the familiar voice came on the line.

"Hello." Joan hoped it was Henry on the other end of the telephone.

"Honey, I tried but there isn't an available flight for three more days." Henry stated with disappointment in his voice. "I wanted to be there sooner."

"Not even the Puddle Jumper?" Joan asked with a whining tone.

"Not even the Puddle Jumper! I decided I would drive. I can get there faster than to wait for the airlines. I just hate the lonely trip across Nebraska without some company. More than anything, I miss my girl." Henry declared with love in his voice.

At his sweet words, Joan started to cry again. She missed him so much. "Ok, dear. But be careful. I heard on the news that is might snow. It's supposed to leave several inches with high winds."

"This is South Dakota, we have snow all winter." Henry stated sarcastically. "The roads are consistently plowed. I will be there as soon as I can, honey. Please pray for my travels and I will keep praying for you and your family. I forgot to ask, is your sister there yet?"

"Yes, Lisa came down from Longmont. She arrived about a half hour ago. We plan to stay at Dad's as long as we are needed. Bobby has agreed to watch the kids so Lisa can stay. The kids are teenagers and just need to be kept out of trouble. Bobby can handle that. Lisa said Bobby had to work so he really couldn't leave right anyway. "

"I love you," Henry passed a kiss in smacks across the telephone line. He thought he would be in Denver by late evening if all went well.

"I love you, too, dear. See you late tonight. Call me if you aren't going to make it so I won't worry."

"I will. Don't worry! I'll be fine. Tell Lisa and your Dad hello for me. See you soon."

With the telephone placed back in its cradle, Henry's mind began to race. He needed to call his boss and his secretary, Marge, to have her reschedule his appointments for the rest of the week. With the approval of his boss, Henry would have his calendar cleared for at least 2 weeks. If Paul died, Henry would need time for funeral arrangements. Joan and Lisa would need help to settle Paul's affairs. Henry had been through this before with his own parents and Alice. He knew there would be an enormous number of items that would need attention.

As Henry walked out to the car with a suitcase under each arm, he noticed the wind was stronger and colder. There was a cloud bank building to the north. Maybe Joan was right, they were expecting snow today. As a precaution, Henry threw a snow shovel and chains into the trunk of the car as well as extra blankets and a pillow. Never a bad idea to carry those items in the winter months of South Dakota, Nebraska, and Colorado, he thought.

By the time his car was fully loaded, he had called their daughter, Brittney, to inform her about her grandfather's condition. He had given his final instructions to Marge. The snow was beginning to fall. Henry made a mental note to check the mail before he left the driveway. Henry decided to call the newsboy and have him hold onto the newspapers until he returned. In case it snowed, he didn't want a pile of wet papers to form on the front porch. Henry would just pay the boy extra for the additional service. Henry noticed his next door neighbor out in the driveway. He asked him to collect their mail from the mailbox until Henry and Joan returned home. With those two items completed, Henry was ready to leave.

The flakes of snow were small and wispy but falling at a consistent gentle pace. The wind was a greater concern as Henry traveled onto Highway 79 south out of Rapid City. He would keep moving south to Chadron, take Highway 385 on to Sydney. Then catch the Interstate 80 to Cheyenne. From Cheyenne Henry would travel south on Interstate 25 into Denver. Henry gave some thought to stopping in Sydney for a bite to eat. On second thought, he would make that decision as he got closer to the small town. It was snowing harder as he got to the South Dakota–Nebraska state line. The ground was white, but the black asphalt of the highway could still be seen. The snow was blowing and drifting into the ditches. Filling them full until it looked like level ground. Henry had lived in this country for years. He couldn't believe how quickly the snow was accumulating. He began to doubt whether he would make it to Denver that night. He couldn't stop. Joan needed him! He had to get there!

As Henry turned south on Highway 385 leaving Chadron behind him, he noticed a Nebraska State Trooper parked off to the side of the road. Henry was going the speed limit. Seeing a trooper in the side of the road was nothing unusual. The roads were still passible but getting worse. Henry knew it was sixty miles of almost nothing before he reached Alliance. The last farmhouse along the highway was about fifteen miles south of Chadron. From there the farms were a distance from the highway and not within walking distance in a blizzard. The only refuge might be the little town of Hemingford which was off of the main highway several miles.

Henry reached Chadron State Park. A flood of memories surrounded him of camping trips with Joan and the kids. He realized he didn't think to call their son, Mike. No telephones available now. Henry decided he would call Mike the next time he was near a telephone. Henry was lost in his thoughts of the past when he began to notice the snow piling in between the pine trees surrounding the park. The snow was falling gently in the isolated area. The tops of the trees swaying with the winds. As Henry came up out of the valley and moved further south on Highway 385, he noticed the visibility in front of him getting far worse. At the top of a long hill as the pine trees pulled away from the highway, the winds become more intense. It was snowing even harder.

When Henry reached the clearing just past the Job Corp on the plateau called the Table, Henry suddenly saw the blue and red lights of a Nebraska Highway Patrol in front of him. At first, he couldn't figure out what he had done wrong to be stopped. The patrolman had completely blocked to road signaling a road closure. It was apparent no one was allowed to go any further south on 385. Henry assessed the situation. It was an hour before sunset. The snow was falling in large flakes. Visibility was decreasing by the moment. Turning back to Chadron would be impossible. What was he going to do now? He promised Joan he would be in Denver tonight. He hated the idea of being delayed. At this moment, a prayer for God's guidance was declared. Otherwise, Henry knew he would take his frustration out on the State Trooper who was just doing his job.

***

Sargent Chad Brown hadn't been upon the Table very long before he was directing people to the Mills Farmhouse. The first car stopped about a mile south of the Mills farm. He directed the gentleman to the farm-house behind him. The man wasn't happy about being delayed. He said his father-in-law was very ill. He had to get to Denver to be with his wife. Officer Brown was only concerned with the man's safety. To Chad's way of thinking saving lives came before family obligations.

Chapter 3

Bill and Mary Colton

Early March 1977

"Wow! It is really getting cold out there," Bill Colton announced as he stomps his way onto the back porch of their Beatrice home. "By the almanac, it's supposed to storm and get colder. The weatherman on TV last night actually agreed. If it stays this cold the rest of the week, I won't be able to get out in the fields to plant the corn, or soybeans. The ground is just too hard to accept a plow. Truth to tell, I'm getting too old to sit on that tractor when it's this cold. If it doesn't snow, what would you say to a trip to see your mother in Hot Springs, South Dakota? We could have a little mini vacation, just me and my girl. We haven't taken any time away since last fall. What about the first or second weekend in April? That's a couple of weeks away. The snows should be gone by then. We could take a week off and then come back to spring planting. We might as well enjoy some time together. Let's pray about it. If we don't feel at peace about the trip, we simply won't go."

"The crops weren't that good last year. You said we had to cut back on our expenses this winter. I agree we need to see Mother. As you said, we need to make it an item of prayer." Mary said matter-of-factly. She was doing her best to be practical but at the same time wanting badly to see her mother. Her mother's health had been good in recent months. They talked every week or so by telephone. Those calls had to be limited due to the high long distance charges connected with each call. Not to mention, the battles to get Mary's share of time on the party line. She had to be so careful what she told her mother because it would spread as gossip into the rest of their community. Information tended to spread on and off the telephone. Mary wanted to limit the infectious talk.

To keep their budget in check, Mary hadn't spoken to her mother in over a week. Her mother lived off of Social Security, so she had a limited budget too. They called each other as often as they could taking turns so no one had to bear the brunt of the expense. Mary wished they could afford a private telephone line just for the privacy. They just couldn't afford the extra luxury. She decided she would write a long letter to her mother this evening to find a good time to visit her. At least the neighbors couldn't read that!

***

Bill broke into Mary's thoughts. "Honey, you need to see your mother. It would be good for both of you. Besides, once it warms up, I will be kept busy in the fields. You will have the garden to keep you busy." Bill reminded. He wanted a get away as much as Mary did. He always found his own activities while they were in Hot Springs. Bill enjoyed Mary's family for the most part. But he loved the outdoors even more.

He began to think about the beauty of the Black Hills. In the winter, they were magnificent with snow packed on the tops of the peaks. By May, the snows would melt leaving the Hills with a blackened color from the pine trees. The Black Hills were named by the Sioux Indians for their color after the snows melted. Bill enjoyed traveling through Northwest Nebraska. The rolling Sand Hills were far different than the flat farmlands around Lincoln and Omaha. Once upon a time, they were the home of the buffalo. Now, herds of cattle dot the sandy mounds. This tall grass prairie is home to wild turkeys, pheasants, and deer. Antelope can be seen when you travel closer to the Wyoming border. As Bill's thoughts traveled, he began to think about the days he enjoyed hunting in the Sand Hills. The outdoorsman debated about taking his hunting rifle on this trip. He secretly hoped he could hunt pheasants with his brother-in-law in Chadron area. On second thought, he decided that idea was fool hearty. He shook his head when it occurred to him that in essence, he was thinking about hunting out of season. Pheasant hunting is a sport that is legal in the fall. Not the spring when the hens are laying their eggs. The idea of taking the rifle was put to rest. Then he realized he needed to be more practical. A snow shovel and extra blankets were in order for this trip. He chided himself for thinking like an over-grown schoolboy. A trip to Chadron or Hay Springs, Nebraska in the fall made far more sense, then thinking about hunting this time of year. He needed to plan ahead for the hunting license and the additional trip up north.

***

"Dear, what are you thinking about?" Mary asked as she broke up Bill's musings.

"Oh, nothing! It just occurred to me that we need to take a snow shovel and chains with us on this trip. We may run into some weather. You never know this time of year." Bill sighed. He got out of that one gracefully. Mary didn't have to know about the hunting fantasy.

"Yes, you are right. I will pack some pillows, blankets, light snacks, and water, just in case the roads are bad. I hope we don't need them though." Mary learned long ago that it was best to over plan in the winter months. Northwestern Nebraska and the Black Hills were far different from the Beatrice, Nebraska area.

"It is far better to take them and not need them. If we are stranded without those items, it could mean our lives in a blizzard. This is an April trip and we both know the weather can change on a dime. What do you plan to take to your mother?" Bill asked knowing full well Mary had already planned their food in her mind.

"I want to put in some plum jelly for Mother. I told her about our good crop of plums. I bragged about the batch of jelly I made last fall. I should live up to my word and take a couple of jars to her. She wouldn't forgive me otherwise!" Mary giggled like a mischievous child who had just created some kind of trouble. "Are you ready for some lunch, farmer? It will be ready in a few minutes. We have some roast beef left from Sunday dinner. I can make some sandwiches."

"Yes, I'm starved. Let me wash up and I will be right back." Bill could smell the freshly baked bread from earlier in the day. He hoped it was included with the roast beef. Mary was a good cook. Bill knew he was a luck man. He hoped they could get their hands on some chokecherries this fall for some chokecherry jam. It sure would be good on fresh biscuits! Bill's mouth watered at the thought of the tasty treat. He smiled. Another excuse to go up to Chadron this fall. They could hunt pheasants and chokecherries along West Ash Road south of Chadron.

***

The weeks passed quickly for Bill and Mary. They had discussed and rediscussed their plans for their weekend trip to Hot Springs. Getting more and more excited with each discussion. They called the kids and her mother to inform every one of their plans once a firm date was established. Bill had arranged for Larry Reed, a neighbor, to come to the farm and feed the livestock while they were away. Larry was a high school student. He loved to be around the livestock. Rather than money, he preferred his payment in loaves of Mary's homemade bread with some of her plum jelly. A treat that wasn't readily available at his house. Larry would gather the mail and place it on Mary's kitchen table while they are away.

***

The evening before the trip to Hot Springs, Bill came into the house from the barn ready for a hot meal and some television. As he turned on the set, he heard the announcer discuss an upcoming snowstorm in Wyoming. Bill wasn't too worried. The weather predictions weren't very accurate most of the time. He thought they would make it safely to Hot Springs by the time storm came through Northwest Nebraska. If they were on the road by 6:00 a.m. tomorrow, they should be ahead of the storm. It was hard to believe anything was coming. A light jacket was all he needed over his coveralls the entire day. He even removed the jacket when he was stacking bales and working up a sweat from exertion. He hated to disappointment Mary who had been planning this trip for weeks. Bill had been caught up in her excitement. He couldn't back out now. This farmer had savings set aside for emergencies. He decided it would be best to take his secret stash with them just in case they had to stay in a motel in Alliance or Chadron to wait out the storm. That money was to be used for something special for Mary for her birthday this summer, but it was more important that he ensured their safety. That would be the best gift he could give her.

"Bill, are you ready to supper? Mary asked from the doorway into the kitchen. She had a thousand things she wanted to get done. Bill's supper and the dishes were among them. She still had to finish packing her clothes. It took most of the day to get their laundry done. Hanging clothes on the clothes lines required plenty of time to allow the clothing to dry in the sunshine. Fortunately, a consistent wind blow most of the day. After completing the vacuuming and dusting, numerous other chores were finished while the clothes were drying on the line. When the dried clothing was returned to the house, the cottons still had to be ironed. The entire process had consumed most of Mary's day. She had baked cinnamon rolls for her mother along with an additional batch for her sister and brother-in-law. Cookies were baked and placed in Tupperware containers to be consumed on the trip. A wicker picnic basket had been pulled from the garage shelf and cleaned. Then she began to pack it with baked goods.

Bill butchered a cow earlier in the week. Mary and a neighbor spent the last couple of days cutting and processing the meat. The beef was wrapped into small meal sized chunks as steaks or roasts. Some of the fattier pieces were ground and packed into hamburger patties. Each piece of meat was carefully labeled and placed in their chest type freezer for later consumption. The heart, liver, and tongue were wrapped and frozen as well. Most every part of the beef could be used in one way or the other. This processing had been very time consuming for Mary even with some help from her neighbor. Mary wanted to take some of the frozen meat to her mother, so she worked really hard getting it ready.

Mary placed a beef roast in the oven to bake while she completed her housework. Later, the hot slices of roast, potatoes, gravy, and canned vegetables from last year's garden were dished out in small bowls. The table was set for their supper. The leftover roast beef from tonight's meal would be the sandwiches for tomorrow. There were very few places to stop for food between Ogallala, Nebraska and Hot Springs, South Dakota. They would find a primitive roadside park to take a break and have their lunch. They never made this trip without plenty of food in the car. The food from the farm reduced their travel expenses. Their budget wouldn't allow too many restaurant stops.

"Yes, I'm starved," Bill exclaimed as he lifted himself from his reclining chair. He strolled to the bathroom to wash his hands and prepare for supper. "That wind is getting colder and the animals are restless tonight. I think they are spooked by the wind slamming the barn doors. I latched the doors down the best I could.

I know creaking doors don't do anything for me! I get jumpy too!"

Mary chuckled at her husband's joke. She knew Bill was teasing. She could get just as spooked by the sounds of the wind. She found herself becoming uneasy when she learned the cattle were restless. That wasn't a good sign. The animals always knew when a storm was coming. She finished preparing their supper, then sat down at the table to await her husband's return.

***

When Mary finally settled into bed for the night, she was exhausted. The winds were still howling. She prayed they wouldn't have to delay their trip to Hot Springs. Funny how she was tired but couldn't sleep. Her excitement captured her restless mind. She knew she could sleep in the car tomorrow. Bill's snores had moved into a gentle slumber. Since he would drive tomorrow, he needed to get a good night's rest. Mary's mind was racing with the things that needed to be taken to her mother. Had she forgotten anything? She had checked and rechecked her list. Their suitcases with extra clothing were packed and beside the front door. Extra blankets, pillows, snow shovel, and coats were beside the door. Hats and gloves were stashed in the pockets of each coat. A cooler for the frozen meat stood beside the freezer ready to be filled in the morning. The wicker basket was packed with snacks such as potato chips and homemade cookies as well as Mary's homemade bread and plum jelly. Mary thought of other things she could add from her cabinets. Then decided she had to place a limit somewhere. She was running out of room in the car. Mary had to prepare the roast beef sandwiches in the morning and take a drink cooler with water. Oh! She decided she needed to pack some paper plates, cups, and silverware which would be used for their roadside picnic. Several hours, and several bathroom stops later, Mary finally settled down enough to go to sleep for a few hours.

***

The alarm clock woke them at 4:00 a.m. Their feet hit the floor. The Coltons were off to the races! Bill dressed and went out to feed the livestock. Mary dressed, started their breakfast, and finished packing the last of the food. She double checked everything again then remembered the paper goods. By the time Bill returned to the house from the barn, the coffee was ready, and breakfast was on the stove. Bill put several eggs in the refrigerator after his visit to the henhouse. He wrote a list of chores for Larry. Bill left the list in the center of the kitchen table beside the loaves of bread and jars of jelly, Mary made for the young man's consumption. Bill decided if the list was beside the bread, it wouldn't be missed. The farmer wanted to be sure the eggs were gathered, the cows milked and turned out to pasture along with the horses.

The sheep would need to be checked and given extra hay. Feed would have to be scattered for the chickens after the hogs were slopped.

After a quick breakfast clean up, Mary put her house in order. They loaded the items from the couch into the car. Bill packed the car tightly to avoid any shifting cargo. With careful planning, he could take an amazing amount in that little car. He knew Mary would provide plenty for him to pack. She always did!

"Why do you clean the house before we leave? Shouldn't you just wait until we get home," Bill asked. He just didn't understand his wife's ways sometimes.

"No, dear! It won't seem like a vacation if I have to come home to a dirty house when I'm tired. I like to be able to rest after we have been gone." Mary stated with exhaustion in her voice. Men don't understand women, Mary thought.

Bill finished packing their old 1965 Plymouth Fury. The car was beginning to look ratty Bill thought but it was reliable and would get them to Hot Springs and back. It was fairly easy on gasoline. Bill admired its sporty look. Mary objected when Bill purchased the car a few years earlier because it wasn't big enough for very many passengers. Since the kids are grown and they weren't keeping foster children, the Fury was the perfect travel car for them. There was room enough around Mary's legs for the basket of food and the small cooler of water. They were pretty well loaded with the rest of the items in the backseat and trunk. Bill had made sure he packed the snow shovel and tire chains on the top of everything else. He didn't want to dig through the contents of the trunk in the middle of a snowy highway.

"I just hope this car is loaded down enough to keep us on the road!" Bill joked as they pulled out of the driveway and headed toward Highway 2. They would catch Interstate 80 near Lincoln to Ogallala. He knew they had an eight to nine hour drive ahead of them. The time changed at Ogallala to Mountain Time which added to their travel time.

***

Bill smiled at his traveling companion as she slept most of the way on Interstate 80. The smooth road made sleeping easy for her. Just as soon as Bill turned north at Ogallala and started up the rougher road toward Highway 385, Mary woke up.

Bill pulled into a service station north of the Interstate to fill the tank with gasoline. "Please fill the tank with regular and check the oil." Bill instructed the awaiting attendant. Mary got out of the car and walked around to the side of the building looking for a restroom. Bill went inside the service station with the same task in mind.

The young man popped the lid to the gas tank open, placed the nozzle into the hole, and started the gasoline flowing into the tank. He grabbed a squeegee and clean rag to clean the windows. When the nozzle on the gas tank snapped to indicate the tank was full, the young man removed it from the car just was Bill and Mary returned to their vehicle.

"That will be $10.58, sir. The price of gasoline just rose to $.62 cents per gallon yesterday. To make matters worse, a loaf of bread went up to $.45 and a gallon of milk is $.75. It's really getting expensive to live, isn't it?" The young man stated. Bill shook his head. The price of gasoline was getting out of hand, he thought. Since they lived on the farm, their milk was provided by the milk cows. Mary made their bread, so they only felt the price of flour if it rose. Bill wondered how long it would be before gasoline was a dollar a gallon!

Bill handed the young man $11.00. "Thank you so much. Just keep the change. Have a blessed day." Bill stated as he started the engine to pull out of the station. He didn't want to wait for the attendant to return with his change plus he liked giving tips when he could afford them.

Bill's stomach began to rumble. He was getting hungry. He would enjoy one of the sandwiches peeking out of its wrapper at Mary's feet. He found a roadside park that overlooked Lake McConaughy just north of Ogallala. This was the perfect place for a picnic and a chance to stretch tired backs and legs.

As they excited the car, Bill noticed the heavy cloud bank to the north. The wind was getting colder and stronger. Mary started to unpack their picnic lunch. The strong winds made the couple decide a picnic lunch inside the car was in order. Bill saw Mary's point but really wanted to be outside of the car for a little bit. He walked around the car several times to get the circulation back into his legs while she prepared their sandwiches on the dashboard of the car.

"Did you see that cloud bank, Mary. I'm concerned about the weather. I don't think we should stay here very long. If there is a storm coming, I would like to get to Alliance or Chadron before it hits. If worse comes to worse, we can get a motel for the night while the storm passes. Those clouds are really dark." Bill's voice was shaky, and Mary could tell that he was worried.

"I agree, honey. I sure hate using our savings for a motel though. A stay in a motel is a good option." Mary stated as she repacked the remainder of their picnic lunch. "I will be ready to go in just a minute."

***

Soon, they were back on the road. The further north the couple traveled, the darker the clouds became. By the time they got to Alliance on Highway 385, the snow was consistently falling. The roads were still drivable even though the ditches were beginning to fill with blowing snow. Bill thought they could easily make it to Chadron before the full force of the storm hit. They proceeded further on their journey. The closer they got to Chadron, the more intense the storm. The snow began to accumulate on the highway. The ditches full of blowing and drifting snow. It was hard to tell where the road began, and the ditches ended. Only the lines of wooden snow fences designed to keep the snow from drifting onto the roadway were visible. At times the wooden fences were replaced by rows of evergreen trees planted along the road to make a natural snow fence. Bill knew by the signs of civilization that they had to be getting closer to Chadron.

Suddenly in the middle of the highway, Bill thought he saw the flashing blue and red lights of a Highway Patrol car. Bill slowed their pace even further. Not sure what he was seeing, he didn't want to have an accident with a patrol car in the middle of nowhere. The snow was falling so hard, he had to use the windshield wipers to keep the window clear. The swishing of the wipers echoed into the little car. Their visibility declined. Both Bill and Mary concentrated on the road ahead of them, hoping to see a clear path. Each praying for God's guidance and their safety. They came to a gentle stop when they saw a gentleman in a State Patrolman's uniform standing before them. God had given them an angel of mercy to protect them in this storm.

Chapter 4

David Abrams, Jason Lee, and Norman Gray Chadron State College Students

⌦

Early April 1977

D avid Abrams reached across his dorm room to his desk in the corner. He needed his history book. He had an exam at the end of the week. History wasn't his favorite subject even though Professor Fairfield tried to make it interesting. David simply preferred his biology classes. He was a pre-med major. He knew he had to pass this history class to have enough credits to graduate from Chadron State College. He would attend Medical School at the University of Nebraska in Lincoln next fall. He had to crack down on his studies to make his dream a reality. His ability to concentrate on History right now was near zero. He really needed a break from studying. David looked around the room for a diversion.

Then, he decided to tap on Jason Lee's dorm room door to see if Jason was interested in going to get a beer at the Favorite Bar downtown. David, from Bismarck, North Dakota, and Jason, from Deadwood, South Dakota, were both over 21. They became instant friends when they arrived at Chadron State College in their freshman year. Depending upon who the bartender was at any given night, The Favorite Bar was known for checking student ID's. They normally didn't allow underage drinkers. As David came into Jason's room, he noticed that Norman Gray was in the room. Norman, from Valentine, Nebraska, was fun to be around but more than a little naïve. David enjoyed testing Norman's maturity. He was easily fooled, but a good sport.

"Hey, do you guys want to come to The Favorite Bar with me?" David inquired. "I could use a break from studying. A beer would really hit the spot."

"Sounds really good to me," Jason said as he grabbed his jacket from the back of his desk chair. "I'm ready!" Jason loved any excuse to get out of the dorm.

"Norman, do you want to come along? I thought you might like a break too." David invited giving Jason a wink. Jason smiled. He knew Norman may be in for a teasing.

"I don't know if I should. They will card me and I'm underage." Norman admitted with frustration in his voice. "I'm always too young for everything! Just wait until I'm 21! I guess one way or the other, I still have 10 months to wait unless Nebraska changes its drinking laws sometime soon. I'm old enough for the military but not to drink in most states. Doesn't make sense to me!"

"Oh! Come on," Jason coaxed. "If they card you, just order a coke. Besides, I want to talk to David about The Klink's concert in Denver weekend after next. Maybe we can talk him into going with us." Jason hoped to talk David into taking his car. It was much more reliable and comfortable then Norman's old clunker.

Jason hadn't been able to purchase a car. His parents didn't think he needed one since Chadron was such as close knit community. Jason's father felt he could walk downtown. The college campus was only as few blocks from the main business district. Jason, like most of the students, lived in the dorms. Meals were provided in the cafeteria above the student union. They could mail letters in the student union post office. The only reason to walk downtown was to obtain personal items such as soaps, magazines, or specialized snacks.

"What's this I hear about a concert," David asked as they walked to the elevator in the High Rise dorm. "How about giving me the details?" They entered the elevator. Jason placed his finger on the control panel and pressed the number 1 to take them down to the ground floor where Norman's car was parked.

"The Klink's concert is Friday night, the 22nd, at Regis College Fieldhouse in Denver. I thought it might be fun to leave a couple of days early so we have time to explore some of the local sights. Maybe go up in the mountains do some skiing." Jason's plans were growing larger by the moment. Norman's simple idea of an evening concert quickly turned into an adventure of epic portions. "We could even go on up to Pike's Peak for a climb before we came back."

"Pike's Peak in the middle of winter! Are you out of your mind, Jason?" David thought his friend was heading to the deep end of the pool. "The concert isn't a bad idea though. We could leave on Wednesday after our classes are over. Find a place to stay in the Denver area, explore the city on Thursday and Friday. It will be very late when the concert is over, so we will have to drive back to Chadron on Saturday morning. It's warm enough that we could camp to save money. I know a campground with shower facilities near Longmont that would be prefect. We can take sleeping bags to keep warm at night. Anyone have a camping stove to cookout?"

Jason and Norman looked at each other and shook their heads. Camping equipment wasn't something they kept in their dorm rooms. They weren't very familiar with camping. It sounded like fun.

"Maybe we can borrow one from someone," Norman suggested.

"If you start asking around for stuff, you will get other people involved. Our secret trip will turn into a group event." Jason said sarcastically. He wanted this to be a trip for three. Besides they were skipping some classes. They would have to lie enough to get away from campus.

"Oh? Yah," Norman stated flatly. He hadn't thought about the consequences of their actions. "Well so much for that idea! It was good while it lasted! I don't suppose there's a place in Chadron to rent such equipment."

David looked at Norman as if he had suddenly sprouted 2 heads. "There aren't any pawn shops in Chadron, so renting is out!"

"But…," Jason declared, "What about the second-hand store down on Second Street? We might be able to purchase what we need! It might be worth a stop to check it out!"

"I hope their prices are cheap. We don't have very much money to spend on this trip." David reminded the other two boys. As it is, the boys would have to pool their financial resources.

As they parked in front of the Favorite Bar, Jason looked across the alley wondering if the second-hand store was open this late in the afternoon. Oh, Well! He was hungry and thirsty right now, that can wait.

The boys found a booth in the side corner of the bar. Jason noticed a Sioux Indian family sitting over in the corner. He smiled at them only to have a girl about 12 or 13 return his smile. She was going to be a beautiful woman someday, Jason thought.

The young man looked the other way directing his attention to his friends seated across from him. The bartender came over to take their orders. He insisted on checking the IDs of the trio. Norman wouldn't be allowed to purchase the beer that he wanted. Just his luck!

"What do you want? Grilled cheese is our special tonight." The bartender offered.

"I'll have a BLT with fries and a coke," Norman piped up. After he thought about what he had said, he looked at the tabletop feeling more than a shy little boy. His efforts to be a man weren't working too well right now.

"I'll have a hamburger with everything, and fries sounds good to me. Please make the burger well done." David announced. The smell of cooking food waffled into the rest of the bar. His stomach rumbled. Food with his beer sounded like a great idea.

"I'll have the same," Jason proclaimed. David could have bet Jason would copy his order. That seemed to happen 9 times out of 10. Sometimes Jason could really be annoying.

By the time the orders were complete, the Indian family walked out of the bar heading for their car in the street. The man in the group got behind the steering wheel. Jason hoped he was sober enough to drive since it appeared, he had drank several beers before leaving the bar. The young man wanted to say something but knew it would just cause trouble. He turned his attention back to his friends.

The boys excitedly discussed their trip to Denver while they waited for their food. The more they talked, the excited they became.

"Why don't we go over to the second-hand store after we eat? At the very least, we can window shop. I'm curious!" Jason declared. He just wanted to see what the second-hand store carried. Jason knew one man's junk was another man's treasure.

"Who has sleeping bags? Does anyone have camping cook ware? We could just build a fire and forget the idea of a camp stove." David suggested. He had been camping with his parents many times. In designated camping areas, there were fire pits that could be used. Just pots and pans to cook their food would be needed. If they wanted a cold camp, then they could eat sandwiches, chips, and cookies. Cooking food was sometimes a lot of work, but a hot meal over a campfire sure tasted good after a long day. David remembered some of the meals his mother used to fix when they went camping. Hobo dinners, hamburgers with everything, smores for dessert were some of his favorites. He wished he knew how she made cherry cobbler. That was the best stuff!

"I have a sleeping bag and cooking ware," Norman piped up. He was finally relieved that he could meet David's needs. Contributing to the campout was important to Norman. He liked to pay his way. The camping gear was a Christmas gift from his grandfather but hadn't been used yet.

"So, do I," David stated relieved that they were making progress in this discussion. "We will need to stop at Safeway or Decker's for bread, sandwich meats, chips, etc. for a cold camp. If we plan our menu, we should have plenty of food to eat along the way."

"I will still need to talk to the gentleman at the second-hand store about a sleeping bag and cookware. If they don't have them, I can buy them at Coast to Coast. Let's plan our menu! Anyone have a pen and paper?" Jason asked as they ate their sandwiches and fries delivered by the bartender. Always practical Norman pulled a piece of folded paper from his hip pocket. David had a pen in his shirt pocket. They were set. By the time their supper was consumed, the menu for the campout was completed.

When the boys left the bar, they were ready for their new adventure more than a week away. Time would go quickly. They had a lot to do to prepare for the trip. No one considered the work they had to complete for their college classes. Their only focus was the trip to Denver.

***

The young men didn't see much of each other for the next week. They were afraid to do too much planning in the dorm rooms for fear of being overheard. The trio met the evening before their adventure to finalize their plans. They had agreed to take David's newer model car since it got better gas mileage than Norman's old car. Comfort was a consideration for that long of a journey. Five hours in a car was a long time if you weren't comfortable. They packed most of their gear in David's car that evening. Everyone was ready! No one checked weather reports or the news. They just didn't see a need.

After classes that Wednesday afternoon, the boys met in front of the High Rise Dorm. By the time the last of the camping gear was loaded, they didn't have a great deal of extra room. If anyone from the dorm asked, they were going out to the State Park. They didn't think anyone would guess they had other plans. What the trio didn't count on was the falling temperatures that morning or the increasingly bitter winds. Since the weather in Chadron was often different from the Denver area, they didn't consider the indications of a pending storm to be a factor. They were going to Denver and that was that! The boys stopped at Safeway for the food items they needed. Packing the paper bags of food around the camping gear. They didn't have a cooler or see any need for one. In a last minute decision, David decided they needed to stop at Donald's Drive Inn for some burgers, fries, and malts. It was snowing hard enough, that David didn't notice Jason getting out of the car and walking into the Donald's Liquor Store next to the Drive-Inn. By the time the girls at Donald's Drive Inn had completed their orders, Jason was back in David's car with a 12-pack of Budweiser and a pint of Peppermint Schnapps. Jason thought the beer would taste good while they were camping that evening. He had heard about the taste of the Schnapps and wanted to try it.

"You are going to get us into trouble," Norman sputtering when Jason got back into the car. He just knew that having alcohol in the car with a minor would get them into trouble. He could feel it coming!

They were still arguing about the purchase of the alcohol when David returned to the car. He passed out the food to the other two boys. David eat his sandwich and fries while they were parked in the parking lot to make it easier to drive. It wasn't long until the trio drove out of Chadron in the blowing snow. David listened to the other boys argue until they started to head south on Highway 385. He noticed the Nebraska Highway Patrol car parked on the side of the road near the Tenth Street entrance. No flashing lights, but they were assembling highway barriers. The patrolman didn't offer to stop David's car, so he went on passed them.

"Hey, guys," David raised his voice in hopes of changing the subject and getting the boys attention off their argument. "I wonder what's going on with the Highway Patrol. It's snowing pretty hard. Are they getting ready to close this road?"

"Who knows? Let's just keep going." Jason insisted. He didn't want anything to interfere with their adventure. Snow wasn't a big deal to him. They were prepared. He knew David always carried a snow shovel and tire chains in his car. "I don't see a reason to stop unless they stop us."

"My thoughts exactly! This storm shouldn't last too long!" David sounded more confident than he felt. The snow was really coming down. If it was too bad by the time, they got to the state park, they could always turn around. He sure hated that idea though.

Just after they passed Chadron State Park and headed up the steep incline to the Job Corp, David spotted a semi coming down the hill on the opposite side of the road. The speed of the semi was startling. Its massive frame was swerving from side to side. David held his breathe as he passed the behemoth in front of them. The semitrailer come within inches of David's front bumper throwing powdery snow on David's windshield. For a few seconds, visibility was cut to zero. When David could finally see the road again, he let out his breath, unaware he had been holding it in the first place. Jason and Norman looked out the back window of the car just in time to see the semi swerve the opposite direction. Suddenly, the massive vehicle was laying across both sides of the highway blocking any possible passage from either direction. Different sizes and shapes of canned goods were thrown out of the trailer landing on pillows of drifted snow. Debris was scattered everywhere. The road will be impassible for hours, Jason thought. David sent up a prayer of thanks to the Lord. The semi could have crushed on them. It was a close call.

***

Sargent Chad Brown had just ended his call on the police radio with Captain Kyle Jacobson. There had been a tractor trailer accident on the steep hill north of the Job Corps. It would take hours and hours to clean up in this blowing and drifting snow. To Officer Brown's surprise a vehicle traveling south out of Chadron came up to the top of the Table. They must have gotten past the Job Corp about the same time the semi came down the steep hill. The two vehicles had to have passed one another. This should be the last car traveling south to Alliance, Chad thought. The roads must be getting very slick because it took this car to long time to come up the hill past the Job Corp. Chad put on his overhead lights to alert the vehicle. The car ahead came to a gentle stop.

The officer exited his vehicle and walked over to the approaching car. He signaled the driver to roll down his window. The driver willingly complied by grabbing the hand crank to make the window descend into the car door.

"Did we do anything wrong officer?", the young man asked. David Abrams wasn't experienced dealing with police officers. He tried to stay on the right side of the law to keep his strict father off of his back. David certainly didn't want his parents finding out about this trip. He didn't need to do something stupid to get himself into trouble.

"I'm Sargent Chad Brown of the Nebraska Highway Patrol," Chad announced. He could see the three young men in the car were more than a little scared. "The road over the Table and through the Sandhills is closed due to blowing and drifting snow. Due to a semi accident, just north of here, the road back to Chadron is closed as well. You will have to stay in the farmhouse to your right until the storm clears and the highway is opened again."

"I know, the accident was awesome! We saw the semi swerve one way and then the other before their load shifted and the entire trailer turned over. The semi appeared to be heading to Safeway in Chadron. Anyway, cans and produce are scattered everywhere! It was cool!!" Jason Lee described with the enthusiasm of a young boy from the passenger seat. "The highway is completely blocked. It's going to take them hours to clean that up. The turned over trailer looks like a beached whale who has given its all! It was scary too! I hope the driver wasn't hurt!"

Chad had to smile at the description. He shook his head hoping the driver wasn't hurt either. The accident certainly ended any more traffic coming from the north. The officer was torn because he couldn't leave his post on the Table to help with the accident. Now his job amounted to stopping cars from the south before they ran into the semitrailer in the blinding snow. He wouldn't be able to go back home tonight either. Chad would have to call dispatch. Maybe someone will call his wife in Chadron to tell her he won't be home tonight. The officer wished he had the means to call his wife privately. The car radio didn't correspond with the public telephone lines. Chad didn't think his CB would work this far away from his wife's unit. He was stuck up on the Table along with a house full of other people. He prayed the county would be able to plow the roads quickly after the storm ended.

"As I said earlier, you will be staying in the farmhouse to the right. They are expecting you. Mrs. Mills wants you to provide any blankets or pillows from your car to make your stay more comfortable. You may be there a couple of days depending how long it takes to open the roads." Chad instructed. He lifted his right arm to point to the small white house hidden by the falling snow.

"Oh! We don't have any," Norman Gray stated, "Blankets I mean! We have sleeping bags!"

"That will work! Take your sleeping bags and pillows with you along with anything else you might need. I'm sure Mrs. Mills can help you. Go on to the house. Knock on the front door. Someone will let you inside." Chad stated precisely as he left the older model Mercury. He was trying to keep the sarcasm out of his voice. These guys didn't have a clue! Just young kids out on an adventure. The trio shouldn't have even been out on the highway in this storm. They will grow up eventually, if they didn't do something stupid to kill themselves in the meantime. Experiences have a way of making people grow.

Chapter 5

George Sims, Brandy, Ethan, and Rick

∞

Mid-April 1977

George Sims sat sprawled out on his living room couch in Frankfurt, Kentucky. As he pulled himself off of the sagging couch, he slid his feet across the floor. The lazy man moved a collection of potato chip bags, cookie wrappers, take-out food boxes, and beer cans to make way for his journey to the kitchen. He would make Brandy clean this place the next time he was allowed to see his kids. She had to be good for something other than having illegitimate children. "I sure could use another beer but I'm out of money. I'm tired of this crap. Not having the money, I need to buy what I want!" George announced to the airwaves. It never occurred to George that a job would solve his financial problems.

He scratched his backside as he wandered into the kitchen. With each step, he shuffled additional debris. Opening the refrigerator door, he cussed. The results were worse than he imagined. The refrigerator was empty except for one empty beer can. It smelled of rotten food and hadn't been cleaned in years. George thought that cleaning the house was women's work. He hadn't had a women in the house since Stella passed away 4 years earlier. She was a good women who gave him two children, Brandy and Rick. Even thinking about Stella now, George began to miss her. He would never have married her, but he still missed her company from time to time. He found himself angry with Stella for leaving him in this mess. How dare her leave him to care for those brats. Those kids were totally worthless in George's view. They didn't even stick around to clean his filthy house. The only thing that really mattered to George Sims was his next can of beer to satisfy his cravings for alcohol. He would have to have more beer soon. He was starting to get the shakes.

Since the state took the kids a year ago, he didn't get a welfare check anymore. He sure would like to have those kids back to take care of him and this house. That welfare check would solve his financial problems. He would have regular money coming in, again. Those paper food stamps went along with the checks. They could be traded for beer if you talked to the right person. That stupid social worker kept saying he would have to be sober and have a steady job to get the kids back.

Her ideas sounded entirely like too much work to lazy George. He wasn't going to go to work and give up his personal pleasures for anyone. Not even those brats. He certainly didn't want Brandy's baby in his home. He wasn't going to raise her kids no matter what. He didn't need one more mouth to feed even though he could get additional food stamps for the little sprout. George didn't want anyone to find out who that baby's father was. Birth certificates would have to be provided. No way! He didn't stop to think that Social Services already had that information. They would have gotten it when the children were taken into custody.

***

A day or so later, George was walking down the street headed for the nearest liquor store. He had begged a few dollars from a kind stranger on the street. As he walked through the parking lot, he noticed a 1969 Ford Country Squire parked in front of the liquor store. The keys were still in the ignition. He walked past the car and into the liquor store. He purchased his case of beer and walked out of the store. The car was still parked in its previous spot. Sly George looked all around. No one was in sight. In a split second decision, George placed the beer in the back seat and crawled into the driver's seat. The vehicle started easily. Before he even realized what was happening, he was driving the car down the street headed for Interstate 64. As he got partly out of town, he realized that he would need some things from his house. Fortunately, the house was fairly close to the Interstate.

George pulled up into his driveway with the stolen car. On the front steps sat Brandy, Rick, and her baby. This wasn't his visitation day, George thought. Was it? Maybe he got his days confused. Suddenly, it occurred to him that he would have to visit the children, not the children visit him. It became apparent they had run away from their foster home instead of going to school.

"Great! What a time for them to show up," George thought. "The kids would just drag him down. Then again with the brats along, it wouldn't look like he had committed a crime. What idiot would steal a car and drive off with three kids inside. This may work after all."

"Hey Pa, where did you get that car?" Rick asked as George pulled into the driveway.

"I bought it!" George snapped sharply. He felt guilty because he had been caught with the car. "What do you think?" Trying to act as innocent as he could. George didn't realize he was only fooling himself.

"How did you get that car?" Brandy inquired sarcastically. "You never had that much money in your life! Certainly not enough for a luxury car."

"Just you never mind. Why are you here?" George asked with anger in his voice. He didn't want to have to deal with those brats today of all days.

"We escaped the foster home while the old witch wasn't looking. Instead of getting on the school bus, we took public transit to your house," replied Brandy. "They wanted to take Ethan away from me. I wasn't having any part of that business. Ethan stays with me. No discussion! So, we ran away."

"Yeah, they say she isn't a good mother. They think he needs a proper home." Rick stated as if he knew what a proper home really was. "The social worker wants Brandy to put Ethan up for adoption."

"Get in the car, all three of you. I have some things to do today. I guess I will just have to take you along." George wasn't happy about taking the children with him. Although, he didn't see he had any other choice in the matter. Maybe, this was going to be easier than he thought. He would be able to take the kids with him and leave this stupid town behind him for good. They would just make it harder though. George decided they could go to Portland and start over. He had some distant family there who he thought would help him.

On the way out of town, George stopped at a secluded bank. He carefully walked into the bank. Looking around, he realized he was the only patron. There was only one teller at the window. No one else seemed to be around. The would-be robber placed his forefinger in his sweater pocket as a pretend gun, then placed it high enough the teller could see it. The look of surprise and horror on the teller's face was evident. Without hesitation, she reached under the counter and pulled out a stack of bills. She placed the bills in a paper bag and handed the bag to the robber. George didn't even take the time to check the contents of the paper bag. He told the teller to lay on the floor behind the counter. As she went out of sight, he pulled his hand out his pocket and calmly walked out of the bank. Robbing the bank had been easier than George thought. There didn't seem to be a guard in sight. The clerk was so scared, she was very cooperative. He didn't consider that he was being recorded on a primitive movie camera above his head.

In a matter of minutes, he crawled back into the driver's seat of the car. He was back on the road with the children heading out of Frankfurt. He slowed his speed to make it look like it was just any normal day. They were a family going on an outing. They seemed to go unnoticed as they passed several police cars going the opposite direction. Virtually they were invisible in the crowd of cars going back and forth along the interstate. George thought the children in the car throw the police off balance since he was a lone robber. He was feeling pretty proud of himself. He had no idea how much money was in the paper bag the clerk gave him. He would count it later.

Since the car was full of gasoline, they didn't need to stop again until they reached the outskirts of St. Louis. He might not have stopped in St. Louis except the car needed gasoline. The kids needed a bathroom stop. They complained they were hungry. Brandy declared Ethan needed some milk. George needed to make a stop himself. The beer in the back of the station wagon was calling his name. George drove into a late night convenience store parking lot. Taking some bills out of the paper sack from the bank, George placed the money in his sweater pocket. The group entered the store. After everyone selected the items they wanted and needed, George pulled some money from his sweater pocket to pay the clerk. The family gathered their purchases off of the counter and got back into their car. George placed several cans of beer in the cup holders next to him, so they were in easy reach. He would drink them as he drove down the road. He started the car engine, placed the car in gear, and pulled out into traffic. The family was back on the road in a matter of minutes.

***

By the time they reached Kansas City, George was growing too tired to drive. He decided he could get a cheap motel in South Kansas City to spend the night. The bottom floor room of a Motel 6 would do nicely. George took one bed and left the children to decide how they were going to share the other double bed in the room. Brandy took one side of the double bed with Rick on the other side. The young mother placed her son in between her brother and herself. They still had some left over snacks from the convenience store that would do until morning. George refused to spend any more money on food for the children. He would save his money for his beer and gasoline.

The next morning, George awakened Brandy and Ethan by kicking the posts on their bed. Suddenly, Rick was awake. Anger tore through him. He grabbed George's foot. With a sudden jerk, George was laying on the floor with his feet in the air. Brandy wanted to laugh but didn't dare. Her brother was getting stronger. George sputtered and spit as he regained his balance. He pulled Rick by the arm.

"We are leaving in 5 minutes, with or without you. Be ready!" George growled as he walked toward the tiny bathroom adjacent to the bedroom. The kid had some lessons to learn.

No breakfast was offered. George had his beer and that was all that mattered to him. No one else's needs were considered. The children eat a few of the crackers but saved the rest for later. They knew how to stretch their food to last for a few days. This wasn't anything new to them.

Taking Interstate 29 into Iowa, then Highway 2 into Lincoln, Nebraska was a tedious drive. There wasn't any place to stop. George began to wonder if he should have filled the car with gasoline in Kansas City even though he thought he had enough for a while. This car seemed to be pretty easy on fuel, but he wasn't entirely sure. He didn't want to run out of gasoline. Too great a danger of being caught by the state patrol or local police. George maneuvered the traffic to get onto Interstate 80 heading toward Cheyenne, Wyoming. With the gas gauge near empty, he decided to stop in Lincoln, Nebraska. He needed another beer, to stretch his legs, and get some distance from the brats for a few minutes.

"You kids stay in this car. Do not go anywhere! You hear me!" George ordered. "If you aren't in this car when I'm ready to leave, I will leave you here to fend for yourselves."

No one said anything. They ducked down in their seats in fear.

While George was out of the car, Brandy snatched some bills out of the paper bag. Ethan needed more milk. She and Rick were hungry. It was apparent to her that father wasn't going to feed them. Dad would fill the car with gasoline, get his beer, and be gone in a hurry. Brandy asked Rick to watch Ethan. She went into the convenience store for enough food to feed the three of them. The young mother saw her father walking into the store. She wasn't supposed to be out of the car. She took cover behind the counter until her father was out of sight. He would draw attention to them by yelling at her if she were caught. That would be humiliating! If he was really mad, he would beat her.

It didn't take long for Brandy to realize her father had robbed the bank in Frankfurt. The teen was afraid she would be arrested as an accomplice. Then they would take Ethan away from her. George was nothing but trouble. It was hard to love her father and hate him at the same time.

George didn't realize Brandy had gotten out of the car in Lincoln until he noticed additional food in the car about the time they got to Ogallala, Nebraska. "Hey, where did you get that stuff?" George demanded. "Aren't you going to share?"

"You don't share with us," Rick snapped as he stuffed more potato chips into his mouth openly defying his father.

"Give me those, they are mine now," George snatched the chips from Rick's hand swerving the car on the highway. "Stupid kid!"

George suddenly realized that he was going to draw attention to their car with this type of behavior on the interstate. They had to get onto a more secluded road. He decided his best option was to go north out of Ogallala, through the Sandhills, to Rapid City, South Dakota. From there they could take Interstate 90 across Wyoming and into Montana. This was much more open territory. They were less likely to be caught. Crowded cities were more dangerous in George's mind.

As they traveled north, Rick began to notice the increased cloud cover. The cold winds were blowing with more intensity across the open plains. He could feel the dropping temperatures on the car windows.

By the time they reached Bridgeport, Nebraska, it was snowing in gentle flakes. George decided to keep going. Snow was no big deal. The road appeared to be clear. He had driven in snow many times. George increased his speed to seventy. Fifty five miles per hour on these open roads with no one in sight was ridiculous

George thought. No one is going to care about his speed out here.

George didn't slow down when he reached the west side of Alliance even though the speed limit reduced to thirty five for a few miles. About two miles north of Alliance, he saw flashing red and blue lights in his rearview mirror. With a Nebraska State Patrolman on his back bumper, George pulled over to the side of the road.

"Nobody, say a thing," George warned. "I will do the talking." George's knees shook with fear. He just knew he had been caught. His own guilt playing on his mind.

The officer got out of his car. Carefully proceeding along the side of the Sims vehicle, Officer Chad Brown observes the contents of the car.

George rolled down the car window with the crank on the driver's door. "Good afternoon, Officer. Can I help you?" George asked as sweetly as he could muster. Hoping the officer hadn't noticed the beer can sitting in the cup holder next to him.

"Hello, I'm Sargent Chad Brown of the Nebraska State Patrol. Your speed was in excess of the fifty five mile per hour speed limit. I know it's a long way between towns in this area, but you must obey the law. Since you are from out of state, I'm going to issue a written warning. You will not have to pay a fine or appear in court. Just keep your speed at the limit and you will be fine."

"We will Officer. Thank you." George tried to be as sweet and contrite as he knew how. He certainly didn't want trouble with this officer. Once the paperwork was completed, the officer and the Sims family parted ways.

George made sure he kept to the fifty five mile per hour speed limit until he was well out of the sight of the officer. Then he took his speed up to seventy. He didn't think the officer would know the difference anyway.

***

The road sign said Hemingford 6 miles to the left of Highway 385. George couldn't see a town from the road. The only buildings in sight were a row of grain elevators paralleling the railroad tracks which paralleled the highway. The elevators were huge. Rick stretched his neck to see the tops of the towers with snow falling gently between them.

"I wish there was a town here, I could sure use a bathroom." Brandy stated.

"Well hold it." Her father growled.

"I can't Dad, I need to stop now!" Brandy whined.

George swerved the car into the large gravel driveway and stopped abruptly. Brandy wondered how she was going to take care of her business out in the open like this with the winds blowing snow everywhere. "But Dad, how?"

Before she could say another word, George got out of his side of the car, opened the front and back passenger doors, and pointed to the ground. "Just squat right here! It's all we've got!"

George didn't notice the lone Nebraska State Patrol car pass them on the highway headed for Chadron.

Brandy did as she was told. Rick relieved himself after Brandy completed her business. George grabbed several more cans of beer from the back hatch of the car. He wasn't going to stand out in the cold very long. Three car doors slammed simultaneously.

The sudden gush of cold wind in the car awakened baby Ethan. He screamed at the top of his lungs. Brandy turned sideways in the car seat to change his diaper with her cold hands. Ethan screamed even louder from the shock to his little legs.

"Can't you get that kid to shut up!" George growled. "Jab a bottle into his mouth." Brandy did just that. Ethan's mouth was so full, from the nipple of the baby bottle, he silenced immediately. His mother was very relieved. She didn't want to anger George. Brandy completed the diaper change and wrapped her son in his blanket to keep him warm. As George pulled out of the parking area, the only evidence the family had been on the paved area were car tracks and two yellow puddles in the snow.

***

The next road sign read Chadron 40 miles. The snow fell even harder. The winds blow white powder in all directions. The family kept working their way north to Chadron with the winds pushing on the car away from their destination. George had to really work it keep the heavy car on the road. The ditches were filling with snow. In places he couldn't see the asphalt pavement. The further north he traveled the worse it got.

As George reached a flat plateau area, the winds were even more intense. Through the blowing snow, he thought he saw blue and red lights. He wasn't sure at first. As his vehicle got closer to the object, he could see a patrol car stretched across the highway. The ditches on either side of the highway were level with snow so he couldn't be sure how deep they were or where they leveled off. George decided he shouldn't run from the roadblock. If they were arresting him, so be it! George recognized the patrolman getting out of the car. It was the same officer who had stopped them two hours ago for speeding. George wasn't sure if this was a good thing or not.

***

Officer Brown rolled his eyes. He recognized the large green car. This was the same driver and kids he stopped for speeding two hours earlier. "Not this guy again!" Chad complained to himself. The Officer didn't know why he was suspicious of this family. Something wasn't right but he didn't know what. He had too many other worries at this moment. He decided he would conduct some inquiries after the storm to see what he could learn. The officer had taken down the vehicle license plate number from Kentucky and the driver's name when he issued the warning ticket. He would have the Captain call the State of Kentucky to run the car tags. Better check for any outstanding warrants on this guy. If Chad's instincts were correct, he was running from something. Chad just didn't have any proof. The driver was certainly nervous. He tried too hard to be cooperative and courteous.

"The road is closed from this point on," explained Officer Brown. "No one is going anywhere until the wrecked semi-tractor and trailer on down the hill is cleaned up." From the reports Chad had received, there were canned goods scattered all over the highway just north of the Job Corps campus on the long steep hill descending into the State Park. Visibility was poor from blowing and drifting snow. They couldn't get a crane into that area to remove the semi until the weather cleared. "No one will be able to travel that road, north or south until the semi is removed from the highway and its cargo is cleared." Chad silently wondered why the semi carrying canned goods didn't stay in Alliance behind the barricades. Giving the driver the benefit of the doubt, Chad decided he may have come through Alliance before the storm got so intense and the barriers put in place. The driver must have thought he could get his load to Chadron before the snow deepened. He must not have known the road, otherwise he wouldn't have been pushing it so hard.

"How long will that take?" George Sims demanded as he pounded on the steering wheel of his 1969 Ford Country Esquire in frustration. He wasn't going to sit and wait in this car with these kids all night long. He wanted to get on down the road before anyone was the wiser. To make matters worse, his supply of beer was gone. He wanted to get to Chadron to replenish his stock.

"Your guess is as good as mine." Chad Brown replied in his stern military voice. Most people didn't complain, but Chad wouldn't give them the opportunity either. He had work to do and lives to save. Complaints weren't on his agenda. This officer didn't have time for unproductive emotional outbursts.

"We are taking people to the farmhouse to the left of the highway. The couple is ready and willing to take guests into their home until the storm passes. You will need to take any blankets and pillows you have from the car into the house. They will be needed to make you more comfortable through the night." With that statement, Officer Brown walked away from the Sims' vehicle. He wasn't going to argue with the man. Mr. and Mrs. Mills would help them get settled.

Chapter 6

Dennis and Louise Fairfield, Susan and Mark

∞

The Morning of the Storm

"Come on everyone, we need to get going if we are going to make it to North Platte for the workshop today," shouted Dennis from the kitchen doorway leading to the carport. Two sleepy teenagers were working their way up the basement stairs barely dragging their feet on the carpeting.

"Do we have to leave so early Dad, it isn't even 5:00 yet. We are up before the sun. Just because we have some dumb girly event for the cheerleaders!" Twelve year old Mark complained as he stuck out his tongue at this sister. She ran upstairs ready for retaliation. "I would rather stay home today than attend this thing. It's dumb!" His voice getting more sarcastic by the moment.

"And what do you plan to do while we are gone all day, son? Oh, I've got it! You want to go to school today, right?" Dennis Fairfield asked in a teasing voice. "We took you out of school so you could support your sister in this competition. She has worked really hard to get this far. The least you can do it be cooperative! Even cheerful!"

"Very funny, Dad," Mark quietly stated as he passed his father in the doorway leading to the carport. He hoped to capture his favorite spot in the backseat of the car.

Just then Susan reached the top of the stairs, she realized she forgot something. "I can't find my other set of pom-poms Mom. Have you seen them? Where could they be?" Susan checked under every piece of furniture in her room. Smiling, Louise comes into the living room carrying both sets of pom-poms in her hands.

"I took them from your room last night to refresh them. They are ready to go, but you need to get your shoes on and find a coat." Louise instructed. She was an excellent mother in Dennis's opinion. He thought his wife did too much for her children. The kids were getting older and needed to assume more responsibility for themselves.

"Are you ready to go, Louise? We need to get on the road." Dennis asked. He hated to be late for anything and preferred to be fifteen to twenty minutes early. Thinking to grab a light jacket from the hall closet, Dennis Fairfield was ready for the long drive to North Platte. The car would be plenty warm.

Louise grabbed her jacket then grabbed jackets for Mark and Susan. Dennis shook his head. Those kids should have remembered their own coats.

"Should we have taken some blankets and snacks with us today?" Louise asked her tall, well -built husband who she thought was the handsomest black man she had ever seen. Dennis was such a kind, gentle person. Louise was very lucky to have met him in college.

"No, we can stop in Alliance for breakfast and find some place to eat in North Platte around the cheerleading clinic schedule." Dennis declared. His wife was always thinking about their creature comforts, but they needed to get on the road. It looked to be a warm day, so he didn't see any problem. This is mid-April. They should have spring weather for the entire trip.

They were headed south of Highway 385 toward Alliance, Nebraska well before the sun shown itself in the eastern sky. They had to be in North Platte by 11:00. They should make it in plenty of time, if they didn't make too many stops. Dennis relaxed in the car seat enjoying the open highway. He loved to drive. It gave him a sense of freedom.

***

At the end of the contest, Susan was very excited. She had placed first in several cheerleading events. Her display of ribbons was proudly hanging on the rearview mirror of the car when Dennis got into the vehicle to start back to Chadron. Louise crawled into her front passenger seat. She gently removed the ribbons. They wouldn't be allowed to hang on the mirror because they blocked Dennis' view when he was driving.

"Why did you take down my ribbons, Mother? Aren't you proud of them?" Susan whined from the backseat. She was tired from a long day of physical exercise. She worked hard for those ribbons.

"Yes, dear, very proud, but we can't let them block your father's view while he is driving."

"All right," Susan huffed.

"Besides they aren't that pretty anyway! Who wants to look at them all the way home," Mark teased. The war between the siblings ignited again. Denise and Louise looked at each other and shook their heads. Will those two ever stop teasing each other?

"I would rather look at them, than you," Susan spouted back. Escalating the war to a greater level.

"That's enough kids. Is anyone getting hungry? I sure am. That looks like a steakhouse over there. Let's give it a try." Dennis stated as he tried to put as much cheer in his voice as he possibly could. He was as tired as Louise and the kids. It had been a very long day. The professor was more than willing to eat and resume the long ride back to Chadron. He would have to teach his History classes at Chadron State College the following day. Louise had taken a personal day from East Ward Elementary school. He was sure her 4th graders would have really missed her.

Louise spoiled those children as much as she spoiled their family.

***

The school district had originally hired Louise for a single year contract. Dennis didn't want to think that was because Louise was black, but it had happened before. As it turned out, the district hired their new teachers with a limited contract. It was a trial period for the district and the teacher. If the new teacher was a good fit, a longer contract was offered the following year. Louise had just signed a five year contract with the district starting the next school year.

***

Dennis found his mind drifting to the history of the area. He loved his position as the head of the history department at Chadron State College. Northwest Nebraska was rich in the history of the Sioux nation. Fort Robinson was a favorite place to visit on his days off. Dennis decided he would like to do more research on Chief Crazy Horse for a future project. Crazy House was killed by a young soldier while he was imprisoned at the Fort. The fort had been the mainstay of the entire area for years. It was known world-wide for training horses as mounts for Army soldiers during the Civil War, World War I, and World War II. During World War

II, attack dogs were trained by the Army also. Both the horses and the dogs were shipped from the Fort with the use of the railroad. One of the most interesting and little known facts about the Fort, is the fact that it housed German prisoners during World War II.

Next summer, the professor planned to spend plenty of time at the Museum of the Fur Trade east of Chadron on Highway 20. They were going to research the founding of Chadron. The location of the city had been moved. The reasoning behind the move wasn't clear in Dennis' mind. So much to learn!

***

As the family turned north at Ogallala, Dennis began to notice it was getting colder outside. The wind had shifted from north to south. The force pushed against the car making it increasingly difficult to keep the vehicle on the road. As they reached, Alliance, the family made a brief stop to use the restrooms.

"Hey, it's starting to snow, Dad!" Mark exclaimed.

Mark loved the snow. It was a new treat to the family. They didn't have snow in Mississippi where Dennis and Louise met in college. In Mississippi, the roads would get icy very quickly, so Dennis was a little nervous at the declaration of even a few snowflakes. Dennis comforted himself in knowing they were driving a 4 wheel drive vehicle. Something his mother made him promise he would purchase when he told his family he was moving to Nebraska.

A few snowflakes turned into a population explosion within a few miles. It was snowing increasingly hard by the minute. The winds blow with great intensity drifting the snow onto the roadway. Louise grew increasingly worried as she gave her husband a look of concern. Snow was not an adventure to her. She was afraid they would get caught in a ditch on the open Nebraska prairie. She had heard too many stories of stranded motorists landing in a snowbank.

Dennis looked away from his wife. He was convinced they had a good car for the conditions. They would be just fine. Dennis kept pushing forward. Hoping to get home before the storm got really bad. Just north of Hemingford at a turn in the highway, they passed a long line of evergreen trees.

"What are those trees lined up along the road for?" Susan asked. She couldn't understand why anyone would plant a row of trees parallel to the highway.

"The farmers and sometimes the highway department plant trees along the roadways at major intersections to keep the snow from drifting up onto the highway and blocking traffic. They are called a natural snow fence. Snow fences can also be made of wood such as those over there, which serve the same purpose," Dennis explained to his family pointing to the wooden fences on the opposite side of the road.

As their 1975 Chevy Blazer passed the last row of evergreen trees, Dennis understood even more the benefits of the natural snow fence. Both the falling snow and the wind intensified. Is this what they meant by a ground blizzard? Dennis thought it possibility was. He reached over to take Louise's left hand to comfort her and to seek comfort from his loving wife. Dennis could tell that she was very worried, but she wasn't expressing her worry to him for fear of alarming the children.

They couldn't be more than thirty miles from Chadron since Hemingford and Chadron are only forty two miles apart. Suddenly, the car shifted in the road. They had just run over a large object. Dennis jerked the steering wheel abruptly to the right to get them back on the road. He overcompensated in the high profile vehicle. The car was out of control on the slick road. It left the highway heading down a steep embankment. The Blazer made an abrupt stop at the bottom of the hill with snow cushioning their blow. Dennis and Louise were facing forward into the dashboard. They were jarred but not seriously hurt. The children were thrown onto the back of the front seats. The contents of the car had flown in various directions. When everything settled, most of the loose materials were on top of Dennis and Louise. Snow covered the front half of the car. It was dark in the cab. They could see some light out of the rear window, but the sun was setting. It would be completely dark very soon.

With panic in her voice, Louise began to feel around the car for the children. "Are you alright, Mark and Susan?" The children were in shock. With a few mons and gronds, they responded to their mother. The children had been asleep. The impact of the accident had awakened them.

"I think so, mother." Was the weak response from Susan. She was too sleepy to realize they had been in an accident. "Where are we?"

"I'm alright, Mom. What happened?" asked Mark. He was laying on his sister's foot. He moved to free her.

Dennis pulled his door handle and pushed on the door frame. The door didn't move. "Well, son, we slid off of the road. We are resting at the bottom of a ravine with snow piled all around us. I can't seem to get my car door open. I think the doors are jammed in place by the impact. Louise, can you move your door?"

She pulled on the door handle, then pushed on the inside of the door. The door wouldn't move. "No, it's jammed too."

"This two door car, our only hope is to crawl out the back window. I'm not sure that's wise considering we are out in the middle of nowhere. Even if I got out of the car, I would have to walk in the freezing cold for help. I think our best bet is to stay put and hope some farmer finds us when the sun comes up in the morning. Let's take inventory. Louise, I sure wish I would had let you bring blankets and extra food as you suggested before we left this morning. We don't even have any water with us. You children wrap up in the extra coats your mother thought to bring for you. Wrap our coats around your legs to keep warm. There is one car blanket in the back. It's not very heavy but your mother and I can cuddle together under it. Mark would you try to reach into the back to get the blanket? Hopefully, our combined body heat will keep us warm until help arrives." Dennis sounded far more confident than he felt. Frankly, he was scared. He hadn't been this scared since he was in the Army in Vietnam. God willing, they would make it through this crisis too.

Dennis examined his watch for the 100th time to check the time which seemed to creep by at an alarmingly slow rate. Hoping and praying someone would find them before they froze to death. Louise and the children had fallen asleep. They had been stuck in this snow drift for the last four hours. His fingers and feet felt numb from the cold. He had never had to deal with anything like this before.

Dennis gave some thought to trying to start the car. He had filled up the gas tank yesterday afternoon at Eitemiller Oil. Those guys were so nice. They always washed the windshield and made sure the tires were inflated correctly. Their friendly attitude and welcoming manner made it easy to return every time the car needed something. The attendant made sure there was plenty of antifreeze in the radiator and heet in the gas tank, so the car was ready for the cold weather. Not every place gave their customers that much attention. In Mississippi, a white attendant wouldn't have even worried about the safety of a black man's car. The professor had referred several of his international students to Eitemiller's station because he knew they would receive good care without prejudice. This was one of the things Dennis liked about Chadron. His family was treated fairly. In his musings, Dennis began to realize that he was getting hungry. It had been almost eight hours since they had eaten in North Platte after the contest. A hot meal from the Chuck Wagon would sure go good right now. Coffee would sure hit the spot!

All Dennis could think about was getting his family back home to safety. They had made some serious mistakes on this trip. They should have taken more clothing, blankets, and some food with them. Looking at it now, Dennis decided he didn't use very good judgement when he bypassed the roadblock in Alliance to come on home. The roads just didn't look that bad to him. He thought they could make it home before storm got very bad. What Dennis didn't realize was that conditions in Alliance may or may not be the same as on the Table south of Chadron. A lot could happen in that sixty mile span. If he made it out of this alive, the professor decided he had some firm advice to give his students about weather preparations on the Nebraska Plains.

Louise began to stir from her spot on the opposite seat. Her hands and feet felt like stiff sandpaper that wouldn't move. "I think I hear something. Someone is coming!"

"Are you sure, dear. You could be dreaming," Dennis corrected. All too afraid his wife was hearing things and would be disappointed when no one rescued them.

Dennis checked the gas gauge on the car again. Thinking maybe they could drive the car out of the ditch with a little help. He didn't know how damaged the car was at the point of impact. He hoped it wasn't too bad since they landed on a pillow of snow. Something had to stop them besides the snow. Dennis had no idea what. He had heard the car hit several items before it rested in its current spot. For whatever reason, Dennis decided to pump the brakes on the car again. He had tried that earlier when he was shifting positions in the car seat. At least, he was working his legs a little bit even though he was producing pain up his legs from his freezing cold feet.

"Yes, listen! I hear people talking!" Louise stated. She was certain she could hear voices above the snow. Then nothing. Was she dreaming? She hoped not. Cold filled her body. She was aware that she would need medical attention pretty soon. She was really concerned about the children. They had been sleeping for some time. Were they alright? She couldn't reach back to feel them even if she tried. Louise didn't know how to deal with this type of fear and helplessness. Exhaustion enveloped her. She was fighting to stay awake. The young mother found herself fighting back tears. She was really scared. Dennis, sensing her fear, wrapped his arm around

Louise's shoulder the best way he could with the console between them. His touch calmed her.

The sound of someone scraping the outside of their car window, made the startled couple jump. The officer wiped away the extra snow from the glass. His flashlight blinded their eyes as he tried to see if anyone was in the wrecked vehicle. The occupants wiped off the frosty windows on the inside of the car, only to find a smiling face on the other side of the glass. Help had arrived at last. None too soon!

Chapter 7

Jay and Annette Mills, Baby Seth

∽

Mid-April 1977

Annette Mills sat on the couch feeding her 2 month old son, Seth. This was the warmest room in the house with a gas stove placed in the corner of the living room. The stove seemed to heat the entire house when the bedroom doors were left open. Annette had just graduated from nursing school the week before. She was enjoying a little more time at home with Seth. She had applied at Chadron Community Hospital to work as a registered nurse pending the results of her state board exams that had been taken a few days before. She grew up on the Table south of Chadron. Annette had attended Highland Center School which was about a mile from her parent's farm. She smiled when she thought about her classmates in the one-room schoolhouse that held grades K-8. She was still in touch with six of the thirteen other students that attended classes with her. The teacher had a lot of patience. She dealt with children in different development stages. Not to mention different educational levels.

Seth quit nursing. Annette put the sleepy baby over her shoulder to burp him before he went down for his morning nap. The infant would sleep for a couple of hours. Annette looked around the room. She really needed to do some dusting and cleaning. Her house-work had been neglected with the completion of her degree and her pregnancy with Seth.

Seth drifted off to sleep on his mother's tender shoulder. Jay Mills came into the farmhouse from the barn. He smiled at his little family. Annette was such a good mother. It was pleasant to see mother and son so contented. With the sudden rush of cold air into the warm living room, Seth lifted his head with a look of surprise. It was as if he knew his father was in the room. Jay smiled. He loved that little boy from the first moment he laid eyes on him.

"Hi, honey," Annette smiled lovingly at her husband of two years. "How are things in the barn?"

"The animals are restless. I think there is a storm coming. Betty is my best weather predicter. She is really cranky this morning. I could hardly milk her without getting kicked. When I listened to the weather on the radio in the barn this morning, they are predicted snow flurries for tonight. It's getting cloudy, the wind has shifted, and the temperatures are dropping. I think it will be much more than a few flurries." Jay walked into the kitchen for coffee and some freshly baked cookies. He was always hungry when he finished his morning chores.

Jay was raised on the Table as well. His parent's farm was a little farther east from Annette's parent's place. Jay had attended the Table Center School which like Highland Center was a one-room schoolhouse with a single teacher. The couple had met in high school in Chadron after they had completed their curriculum at the elementary level in the country schools. Annette lived in an apartment in the basement of a host families' home while Jay lived with his grandparents in Chadron. The thirty miles from the Table to town was too far to travel every day especially when they weren't old enough to have driver's licenses. Host families were needed until transportation was more available. These families were usually relatives or someone close to the family of the high school student. Jay had really enjoyed his time with his grandparents while he was in high school.

His grandfather's health declined before Jay started high school. The old man couldn't farm his land on the Table any longer. He rented the farm out to another family who shared the profits. After five years, the renters had saved enough money to purchase their own land. Right after high school graduation, Jay's grandmother passed away. His grandfather offered the farm to him. Jay wanted to attend engineering school in Rapid City at the School of Mines in the worst way. In the end, he decided that he would try farming his grandfather's land for a few years. He owed his grandparents that much.

Jay and Annette had dated most of their senior year in high school. It was not a surprise to anyone when they were married a year after high school graduation. They decided Annette would attend nursing school while she had the opportunity. Her parents helped her to pay the tuition and some of the expenses. Jay appreciated the extra help. If something happened to Jay, he knew Annette would have the skills to take care of herself and their children.

After settling Seth into his crib, Annette went into the kitchen to rinse out his baby bottle. The breakfast dishes needed to be done and the entire house cleaned. The young mother hoped Seth would cooperate with her plans. As she went around the corner into the kitchen, the wall telephone rang. The sound of its bells carrying through the house. She rushed to answer it before the noise awakened her son.

"Hello, Mills residence, Annette speaking," her soft voice was a welcome note to Captain Kyle Jacobson's otherwise hectic day.

"Mrs. Mills, this is Captain Kyle Jacobson with the Nebraska Highway Patrol. I have been trying to reach you for an hour or so. Your party line is very busy!" He smiled when he heard several clicks on the line. The listeners on the other end of the line got the hint and hung up their receivers. Darn party lines anyway! "We need to ask you a favor. We blocked the highway between Chadron and Alliance due to poor road conditions, but we need to catch the people that got past either road-block. They will need a place to stay for a night, maybe two. Would you have room?"

Annette looked out the kitchen windows down their long driveway. Until now, she hadn't noticed it was snowing. "We will make room Captain. We may have some sleeping on the floors, cots, and couches, but they will be safe and warm during their stay with us. Do you have any idea how many people I could expect?" Annette asked as she mentally calculated food and sleeping arrangements.

"No, I don't. If I had to guess, I would say between 10 and 20. Thank you so much for putting these people up for the night. I hate the idea of leaving someone out in the cold to freeze to death." Kyle Jacobson wished he was available to assist the young couple with their guests. "You should be hearing from Sargent Chad Brown. He will bring the motorists to you as he locates them."

"We know Chad. We met him a few years ago. He's a good man. We are glad to help. We will be watching for your stranded motorists." Annette suddenly found herself panicked. The house was a mess, and she was having company.

Without knowing the number of guests, she would have to be very flexible in her planning. She thought she would plan for about twenty. It would be easier to decrease, then to try to increase at the last moment.

She wanted plenty of food for her hungry travelers. Fortunately, her freezer was full, and they had plenty of canned goods. She could make do with their current provisions. Annette pulled several pounds of hamburger from their freezer. They had plenty of navy beans. A batch of chili soup would feed people as they arrived at different times. She could keep the soup hot on the stove at a low temperature for several hours.

At the rate it was snowing, they would have guests in a matter of hours.

Chapter 8
Entering the Farmhouse

H enry Hapfield parked his car in front of the Nebraska State Patrol vehicle. He could see the officer exiting his car, zipping his overcoat, and placing his wide-brimmed hat on his head.

Henry reached over to the hand crank and rolled his car window down just far enough to talk to the officer but not so far as to let snow into his car.

"Hello, officer. How can I help you?" Henry asked politely.

"Hello, I'm Sargent Chad Brown of the Nebraska State Patrol. We have closed Highway 385 between Chadron and Alliance due to this storm. Visibility as you can tell, is very poor. The blowing and drifting snow has produced a ground blizzard. The temperatures are dropping by the minute. For your personal safety, I can't allow you to go any further. We have arranged for you to stay in the farmhouse just to your right. The young couple expect stranded motorists. They will provide food and lodging until the storm passes. You can pull your vehicle into their driveway. Please get it as far off the road as possible. We don't want it damaged when the snowplows come through after the storm. One other thing, Mrs. Mills has requested any blankets or pillows you may have in the car. She says she will need them to make your stay more comfortable." Chad had the feeling he will give this speech several times this evening.

"Thank you, Officer. One question…Do the Mills have a telephone I can use?" Henry asked. He would have to call Joan to tell her he has been delayed. Henry didn't like this delay in the least. Joan won't be happy about it either. None the less, she would be more concerned about Henry's safety.

"Yes, they do." Officer Brown stated. "You may have to compete with other members on the party line, but you can get your call through."

"Thank you, again." Henry said. Everything in him wanted to scream at the officer but the storm wasn't his fault. Henry was very frustrated by the entire situation.

The officer walked away from Henry's car. Henry reached for the crank on his car door and rolled the window back up into place. He placed the car in reverse backing down the highway a few yards before turning his car into the Mills driveway. He tried to park the car so he wouldn't be pinned into the driveway if it filled up with other cars. Henry decided to place the rear of the car closest to the house. That way, he could exit the car more easily. He wouldn't have to back out of the driveway later when the snow was a lot deeper. At this point, Henry could kick himself. He hadn't thought to put blankets or food in the car. As many years as he had lived in this area, he knew better than to travel in the winter without those basic provisions. Henry kept a snow shovel and chains in the car year around. Men remember those things. It was Joan who thought about their comforts. She would have thought about the blankets and extra food for the trip. He sure missed her.

Henry walked over and knocked on the front door of the little farmhouse. He was greeted by a young woman with long blonde hair and blue eyes. Evidently, a descendent of the German immigrants in the area. She had a warm welcoming smile. The small infant on her shoulder had coal black hair. As Henry entered the house, a loud burp was expelled from the child.

Henry and the young women laughed at once. Glen Campbell could be heard singing, "Gentle on my Mind" from the radio in the kitchen. Just about that time the radio announced the call letters of KLRC, the lone AM radio station from Chadron. Probably the only radio station that could be heard on the Table.

"Hello, I'm Annette Mills. This loud little dude is Seth. I hope he's more comfortable now!"

"I'm Henry Hapfield. The state patrolman told me to come over here to wait out the storm."

"Please, come on in, Mr. Hapfield. Make yourself at home. Can I get you anything? I have soup on the stove for supper. I can offer you some cookies and coffee, if you like."

"Maybe later. I really need to get to your telephone if I can. I will call collect." Henry didn't want to create a long distance telephone bill for this young couple who were being so generous in allowing him to spend the night.

"The telephone is on the wall in the hallway in front of the bathroom. Pick up the receiver and listen before you dial. Just a precaution in case Gladys and Sofia are talking. Usually, this time of day the lines are clear because they are cooking supper for their husbands." Annette stated. She wouldn't be surprised if the curious ladies were listening on the line to learn who Annette and Jay had in their home. Those ladies kept up with the news on the Table! Especially any news that spread on the party line.

"Thank you so much, Annette. My father-in-law is very ill in Denver. In fact, I was headed there to be with my wife. I need to call and let her know where I am. She will be worried if I don't show up tonight." Henry didn't know why he felt the need to make explanations to this young women. The gentleman just didn't want to do anything to appear dishonest.

Henry lifted the receiver from the bracket that cradled it, placed the receiver to his ear, and listened. No other voices. Good! He could dial the telephone without waiting for the others to get off of the line. Henry dialed the telephone number, reached the long distance operator, and ordered his collect call to his wife at her father's home.

"Hello," The male voice on the other end of the line was unfamiliar to Henry. He expected Joan or her sister to answer the telephone.

"I have a collect call from Henry Hapfield. Will you accept the charges?" the operator asked in a monotone voice.

"Yes, Operator, I will accept the call." Henry heard the stranger reply.

"Bobby, Is that you? I thought you were in Longmont." Henry asked when it occurred to him who could be answering Paul's telephone.

"Yes, it's me." Replied Bobby is a cheerful voice. "I'm manning the telephone. The kids and I came down after I got off of work. "I'm not sure if we will stay or go back home later tonight. I work tomorrow and the kids have school. Where are you?"

"You won't believe this! I'm about fifteen miles south of Chadron on the Table stranded in a loving little farmhouse. It's snowing so hard, that it's turning into a ground blizzard. The winds were whipping the car around. I suspect the temperatures are in the teens. A Nebraska State Patrolman stopped me. They have closed Highway 385 both directions. The officer said he couldn't allow me to go on to Alliance for my personal safety. I guess I'm here for the night. Maybe longer. Is Joan around? I would sure like to talk to her." Henry asked. He missed Joan and wanted to hear her voice. Bobby just couldn't fill that void for Henry.

"Joan is at the hospital with Lisa. Paul isn't doing very well. The girls don't want to leave him alone. Would you like me to tell her where you are and why?" Bobby asked.

"Would you please? Tell her I will call her back at her father's place early tomorrow morning. Maybe I will have a progress report by then." Henry said with disappointment in his voice.

"I sure will. Stay safe Henry. Don't do anything foolish!" Bobby instructed.

"Thank you, Bobby! I'll talk to you soon." Henry placed the telephone receiver back onto its hook. He sure wished he could have talked with Joan. Messages between them could sometimes lead to misunderstandings.

As Henry walked back into the cozy kitchen, he noticed someone knocking on the front door. Annette was nowhere in sight. She must have been taking care of the baby. Henry decided the least he could do is give the young woman some assistance.

***

Sargent Chad Brown caught sight of another car traveling north from Alliance. He could barely see them in the blowing snow. Chad flashed the car lights to make himself more visible.

Bill Colton pulled his Fury in front of the patrol car. Rolling down his window with the window crank, he hung his head outside to talk to the officer. "Hello, Officer is there something wrong?" Bill asked confused as to why the road was blocked. The road conditions were beginning to frighten him.

"Hello, I'm Sargent Chad Brown of the Nebraska State Patrol. I have been ordered to close the road until this storm has passed. We have arranged for you to stay at the farmhouse to your left." Bill could barely see the small house through the snow. "They are prepared for overnight guests. Mrs. Mills asked that you bring blankets and pillows to the house with you if you have them. It's my understanding she has enough places for people to sleep but not enough bedding to keep them warm. Go ahead and pull into the driveway as far as you can go. Take what you need to the house. If you tap on the door, they will let you inside."

"Thank you, Officer, we will do that." Bill stated. "Mary this is an answer to a prayer. I was becoming concerned about the roads. I'm getting too old to be driving in blizzards. What do you want to take in the house with you? I will help you gather it all up."

"Blankets, pillows, suitcases with our clothing, and the food basket. Leave the meat and the other stuff. If we need it, we can always come back out to the car later." Mary directed.

"Ok, sounds good. I hope the snow doesn't get too deep before morning. At the rate its falling, it could get to be waist high." Bill stated. He tried to make it sound like a joke, but he knew better.

Just as Bill as about to move the car, a young man in a bright red ski cap and heavy winter coat greeted them.

Over the winter coat, he had an orange reflective vest to make it easier to see him in the blowing snow.

***

"Hi, I'm Jay Mills and I live over there. You can park your car in back of that other car." Pointing to a spot on the edge of the roadway. "My wife, Annette, is waiting for you. Take anything you may need for the night with you because it may be hard to get back out to your car in this storm. It will be dark soon." Jay smiled and made the couple feel welcomed into this unusual situation.

***

Mary began to gather up the items she considered important for a night's stay. She wished she had packed a couple of overnight bags just for a brief stay. She hated to have Bill carry those large bags in the deep snow to the farmhouse. Mary mentally planned to take several pieces of food with her that might freeze in the car. She wasn't worried about the meat. The cold conditions and the coolers would keep the meat well protected for her mother. Mary gathered blankets, pillows, and the food basket and headed to the farmhouse in the snow. She was thankful she wore slacks. Her legs were freezing from the cold wind. She hadn't expected to walk fifty yards to a farmhouse door in the intense wind and blowing snow.

When Mary knocked on the front door, to her surprise a gentlemen greeted her into the warm little home that had been made ready for guests.

"Hello, I'm Henry Hapfield. It appears that the young woman of the house is tending to her baby. Please come in out of the cold." Henry opened the door even wider to allow the woman entrance into the house. Her arms were loaded with a basket, blankets, and pillows. She was ready for any situation.

"Hi, I'm Mary Colton. This is my husband, Bill. We are from Beatrice and headed for Hot Springs to see my mother."

"Pleased to meet you, Mr. and Mrs. Colton. I'm from Rapid City and headed to Denver to see my ailing father-in-law." Henry replied to stay in step with the rest of the conversation. Most country people identify themselves with their homes. Locations are important to them.

"It's Bill and Mary," Bill stated with a friendly handshake.

"I'm Henry." With broad smiles, the three middle aged people became friends.

"Hi, I'm Annette Mills. This little pirate is Seth. Sorry, I wasn't here to greet you, but he had a bit of a personal crisis. His comforts are very important to him."

Everyone laughed at the joke at Seth's expense breaking the tension in the room. He didn't seem to care. Seth was comfortably settled into the crack of his mother's arm.

"You can put those things in the laundry room on the washing machine for now. Mrs. Colton, isn't it? I think we will put you and your husband in there to sleep. Those cots should keep you comfortable and warm. Are those blankets I see? I'm really glad you have them. I have some cots, but not a very big supply of blankets and pillows." Annette talked a mile a minute. Thoughts racing through her head so quickly she couldn't get them out of her month properly. Nervousness did that to her.

Mary liked the young woman immediately. Annette tried to think of everything her guests might need at once. Mary realized she would do the same thing.

"Oh! Don't worry about us, Mrs. Mills. This will work very well. Please call me Mary."

"I'm Annette. It's nice to meet a new friend." Mary thought Annette's smile lite up the room.

"I baked bread yesterday and brought a couple of loaves with us. I thought we could include them with your supper. I even have fresh plum jelly to spread on the homemade bread." Mary declared. Thankful that she included extra bread in her basket of goodies before she left Beatrice. The Lord must have known she would need it, she thought. She was reminded of the story of Jesus multiplying the loaves and fishes to feed a large number of people. Mary felt Jesus was doing the same thing here.

"Homemade bread will make a wonderful treat to have with the chili I have on the kitchen stove. I thought soup was best tonight because people will be coming into the house at different times. I know most will be cold and hungry. Soup always hits the spot. I can open some canned applesauce for dessert along with the cookies I baked this morning." Annette stated. She got the feeling this middle aged woman will be a great deal of help over the next few days. Annette was very thankful for the extra pair of hands with little Seth to care for.

"That sounds perfect. Is there anything I can do? I will be more than glad to help." Mary said with a smile on her face. It was apparent she was accustom to hard work and keeping an orderly house.

"No, thank you! We are good for now. The soup is simmering on low. Would you and your husband care for some of cookies accompanied by some hot coffee? After being out in the cold, I'm sure something hot would be welcomed." Annette asked. She was feeling nervous because she didn't know her guests. The young woman wanted to make a good impression.

After taking Bill and Mary's things to the laundry room, everyone headed to the kitchen for some hot coffee and cookies. Annette turned off the radio. The station would end its day soon. After that all they would hear is static. She invited her guests to sit at the kitchen table. It was the center of activity in this farmhouse.

"How old is your baby, Annette?" Mary inquired. "He's certainly a cutie. I could just cuddle him."

"As you can tell, my wife loves children." Bill stated. "Mary will fall in love instantly with any child."

"Seth is 2 months old. He's beginning to show his personality. It's like his father in one respect. Food is his top priority. He has no patience when it's time to eat." It was evident the young mother adored her son. Annette seemed to take parenthood with love and humor. This little boy is very lucky. He will grow to be a fine young man someday.

"These cookies are excellent," Henry declared.

"Would you like some more?" Annette offered passing the plate of cookies across the kitchen table. "Anyone else? Does anyone need more coffee? There is plenty. I will keep the pot going so you can help yourselves. There are cups in the cabinet above the coffee pot."

"Not right now. I have to watch the waistline." Bill stated patting his protruding stomach.

"Yeah, getting out there where you can see it!" Mary joked. Henry and Annette chuckled but Bill seemed irritated by the comment. Annette guessed it was an issue between the couple that Bill didn't want discussed in front of others.

***

The college students were still shaken by the sight of the police officer. They hadn't gotten past the trauma of the tractor trailer accident. They had been out of Chadron for a couple of hours. In that short amount of time, they had had more adventure than they could imagine. This was turning out to be a day they would never forget.

"Are we really going to spend the night here?" Norman wasn't sure he wanted to spend the night with strangers. What was he getting into? He feared the unknown. The young man had been taught to be careful of strangers.

"I don't see that we have a choice." David stated. "It looks like we will need our sleeping bags and pillows after all. Let's leave the case of beer and Schnapps in the car for later. We can take the groceries from the trunk. I hate to waste the food. I don't think we will be going camping this weekend. These folks might appreciate the contribution to their meals."

"That's a great idea, Dave." Jason's voice sounded more cheerful than he felt. He was really looking forward to going to the concert in Denver. Their campsite would be someone's living room instead of the openness of the Rocky Mountains. Bummer!

David put his car in park and turned off the ignition. He partially removed an 8-track cartridge from the player to keep it from playing while they were out of the car. The boys exited the car. Most of what they needed to take in the farmhouse was in the trunk. Norman didn't follow David's instructions. He slipped the bottle of Peppermint Schnapps in his loosely fitted left jacket pocket. Norman didn't realize the heavy bottle would fall out of his pocket when he reached into the trunk of the car. The snow was falling so hard and heavy, the boys could barely see the little white house in front of them. They had to dust the snow off of their hair, jackets, and sleeping bags when they got to the door of the farmhouse. Jason knocked on the door.

"Well, hello. I'm Annette Mills. Come on it." Annette opened the door up wider to allow the young men entrance into the house.

"You live here?" Norman asked thinking he had found the proverbial farmer's daughter.

"Yes, my husband and I farm this property for his grandfather." Annette replied realizing she wasn't much older that the young man in front of her.

"I'm Norman Gray, this is Jason Lee, and David Abrams behind him. The officer outside said we were to come to you for a place to stay tonight. It that right?"

"Yes, Norman. Your bed maybe your sleeping bags on a cot or the couch but you will be warm and comfortable. I'm glad you brought them with you. This house is very cool at night. You will need them." Annette advised.

"Where do we put our stuff?" David asked looking around the room for a likely spot. "Will the area between the couch and the wall be alright?"

"That will be perfect, David. After you get settled, I have cookies and coffee in the kitchen. I can make some hot chocolate if you don't like coffee. I know you boys must be cold after being outside in the snow." Annette stated. David decided he would follow this girl anywhere. Too bad she was already married.

When the boys walked into the kitchen, Annette introduced them to the Coltons and Henry Hapfield.

"Where are you boys from?" Bill asked.

"I'm from Bismarck, North Dakota, Jason is from Deadwood, South Dakota, and Norman is from Valentine, Nebraska. We are students at Chadron State College. We were on our way to a concert in Denver tomorrow night. Doesn't look like we will make it, though." David stated. He hated the idea of missing the concert, but he couldn't do anything about the road conditions.

"I was on my way to Denver too. I live in Rapid City. My father-in-law is very ill. My wife has been down there for a week already. I was going to join her." Henry informed the boys.

"Where were you going, Mr. Colton?" Jason inquired.

"My wife and I live in Beatrice down near Lincoln. We were headed to Hot Springs to see her mother. We take produce and meat from our farm up to her to help augment her grocery bill. Mary likes to check on Irene in person. This way everyone is happy." Truth be told, Bill liked to check on Irene in person just as much as Mary did.

"These cookies are wonderful." Norman stated shoving another bite into his mouth.

"Save room for supper. It will be ready in about an hour." Annette loved to see someone enjoy her cooking.

"That reminds me. We bought bread, lunchmeat, chips, and cookies to eat on our camping trip. Since we are camping in your living room, could you make use of the food to go with your supper or tomorrow's lunch?" David asked, thinking that was the least they could do for the young couple who helped them.

"That would be great. I was worried the soup I fixed wasn't going to be enough. The Lord has provided a bounty." Annette stated thankfully.

Jason was glad he left the case of beer in the back seat of the car. He felt funny about bringing it into the house around the middle aged adults. It just seemed wrong somehow. If they decided they wanted the beer later, they could always go back out to the car. The cold car was the best place to keep it chilled anyway.

After their snack, the boys settled into the couch at the farmhouse. Annette turned on the television to KDUH-TV out of Scottsbluff. The only television station for miles around. No choice of channels, just one. If you lived inside the Chadron city limits, you could subscribe to cable television from Denver. The cable company didn't offer service this far out of town.

The smells coming from the kitchen were generating hunger pains for the young men. Norman hoped supper would be ready fairly soon. The hamburgers from Donald's Drive Inn and the cookies were fading fast.

***

"I don't like this! I don't want to stay in the stinking farmhouse tonight. How did we end up in this mess anyway?" George Sims asked no one in particular. The children in the backseat of the car didn't respond. They knew better. Their father would retaliate in a manner that wouldn't be pleasant. It was far better to just sit quietly.

"You brats hear me?" No response for the children except their eyes staring at their father. "Take only what you need and nothing more into that house! Don't take any of those crackers or chips with you. Leave it here! Those people don't need to eat up what little food we have. Are you listening to me?" George demanded taking the last sip of beer from the can on the console of the car. The children shook their heads in the affirmative. They wondered what they would eat without the crackers to sustain them.

Brandy reached for the gallon jug of whole milk for Ethan. She would need to feed the infant.

"Leave that milk here. Them people can find something to feed that kid!" George barked.

"Yes, Dad." Brandy replied. She felt very intimidated by her father, when he was drinking. She knew she had to be cautious. She wasn't sure how she was going to feed her son. Ethan, at 4 months, had spit up on the outfit he was wearing after she fed him the whole milk. The outfit reeked of sour milk. She didn't have any other food or clothing for him. All she could do was wrap her son in a thin blanket with a diaper wrapped around his waist. The young mother held her son closely. Rick noticed that she put several packages of crackers from

101

the convenience store in between Ethan and the blanket. He smiled at his wise sister. She was making sure they would have something to eat.

Brandy tried to keep Ethan warm with her body heat as she trotted across the deepening snow to the farmhouse. Rick followed her very closely. He didn't want to be very far from the safety of his sister's protection or her stash of crackers. When she reached the farmhouse, Brandy and the baby were freezing cold. Neither one of them had enough clothing for the biting wind. Rick wasn't much better off with only a thin T-shirt. Neither one of them even owned a coat. They had never experienced the bitter cold of Nebraska.

***

Annette and Mary were appalled by the condition of the children when they were brought into the farmhouse. The entire family was in need of a bath. Their attire was filthy. Annette had never seem people who were so ill kept. She looked over the rough looking man standing before her with distaste. She tried to put on her best face, but it was difficult. "Hello, I'm Annette Mills. Welcome to our home. The man standing behind you is my husband, Jay."

***

Jay had been outside tending the livestock in the snow before it got too dark to see. He made sure there was plenty of hay for the cows and horses. The ewes with new lambs were brought into the barn to keep the newborns from freezing to death in the extreme temperatures. The pigs were slopped, and the eggs gathered. "I guess they are set for the night." Jay thought. He was happy to know they had some new lambs in the last 24 hours to add to his herd. Hopefully, they will bring a good price at the sale barn next fall.

Jay offered George Sims a hand to shake as a greeting. George refused the friendly offer. Jay shrugged his shoulders. This man was definitely didn't know the customs of the area, Jay thought. The young farmer could smell beer on the man's clothing. The man reeked of body odor. His tattered clothing was in need of washing and hung on his body. Jay had never seem someone so ill kept.

***

George turned his attentions to Annette. "You are definitely a pretty one. Got some grub?" George asked. He could smell the soup cooking in the kitchen. "I'm starving!" No introductions of his children were offered or an acknowledgement that they existed. Jay shook his head. He didn't like this man. By first impressions, this man thought only of his own needs. No one else mattered to him. Jay found himself watching his wife protectively. He didn't think he could or should trust this stranger.

***

"Supper will be ready in about an hour." Annette stated. "Please make yourself to home." Then she noticed the children standing behind their father. The young girl was dressed in a knee length dress with a light sweater to cover her shoulders. The younger boy had blue jeans with holes in the knees and a T-shirt that was two sizes too big for his thin little body. Neither child had a coat. The children's clothing was so dirty, Annette wasn't sure of the colors of the fabric. She fought the urge to clean them from head to toe. She was really bothered by the unkept condition of these children. No child should be that neglected. The young mother was well aware she didn't have the right to step in and care for them. She fought her motherly instincts to keep from taking charge of the children in front of her.

"Hi, I'm Annette," she said to Brandy. "Who are you?"

"I'm Brandy. This is my son, Ethan. He's four months old. This is my brother, Rick. He's 13. My father is George Sims. Please to meet you." Brandy said. She didn't seem willing to make eye contact with the young woman. Annette noticed the children watching every move their father made with fear and trepidation in their eyes.

"And how old are you?" Annette inquired.

"I'm 15, I will be 16 in a few months." Brandy stated. She was happy to be acknowledged. The young girl seemed proud of her age not realizing that she was a very young teen parent.

"I have a son, Seth who is 2 months old." Annette stated. She noticed the baby in Brandy's arms was only wearing a diaper. "Do you have any other clothing for Ethan? This house isn't very warm. He will need something to wear." Annette was horrified to see the baby in the middle of winter with only a diaper for clothing.

"No, Mam. He spit up on the only sleeper he had. It was wet and smelled really bad. I left it in the car." Brandy bowed her head in shame. She wanted to take better care of her son and couldn't. It was apparent to Annette that neither child was receiving very good care.

"I bet I have some sleepers that would fit him. Let's see what we can find." Annette's encouraging tone welcomed the children. She drew them further into the cozy little house.

"Thank you, mam. That would be very nice." Brandy looked for her father to object. George said nothing and continued looking around the little house. Jay wondered if the man was looking to see if there was anything of value to steal. Then he chided himself. He shouldn't be so suspicious of other people.

Annette led the children into the smaller of the two bedrooms. "This will be Seth's room when he's old enough to be in here by himself. I thought we could put up some cots. Your family can stay in here for the night.

I'm sorry, we only have one bed in the house. But we have enough cots to keep everyone off of the cold floors. Did you bring any blankets or pillows with you?" The young woman asked.

"No, mam. We didn't have any in the car." Brandy stated. Rick followed closely behind his sister. Annette noticed he seemed afraid to let her out of his sight for a moment. Who knows what these children have been through. They obliviously depend a great deal upon each other.

The young woman opened a dresser drawer and pulled out a light blue sleeper with fabric heavy enough to keep Ethan warm. "Here, this sleeper should fit him perfectly. I will round up some blankets for you from the other bedroom. I'll be right back." Annette left the room. She found the additional blankets along with some pillows in the adjacent bedroom. Her arms were full when she returned to the smaller room. These blankets should keep the Sims family warm for the night, she thought.

When the new sleeper was fitted on Ethan, he was given a fresh diaper. The baby began to look around the unfamiliar room with interest. Annette noticed the infant seemed to have a lot of gas on his stomach. Brandy seemed unaware. The interaction between mother and child was stilted somehow. As if Brandy wasn't mature enough to have a good understanding of her son's needs. What concerned Annette even more was that Brandy didn't have any food for her son.

"Do you nurse the baby?" Annette asked. Thinking if Brandy nursed the baby, then that was the reason she wasn't carrying any food with her.

"No, mam. I use a bottle." Brandy declared. "I left it in the car."

"I see. Do you have any formula for him?"

"No, he drinks regular whole milk."

"Doesn't that upset his stomach?" Annette inquired. Most of the time, whole milk was too harsh for smaller babies.

"I don't know, he hasn't been drinking it very long."

"What was he drinking before you put him on whole milk?"

"I had formula for him when we were in foster care. Dad refused to buy anymore formula when we returned to his house because it's so expensive." Brandy stated. She didn't tell Annette that she and Rick had run away from the foster home or that they had just moved back with their father the day before. What would these people think if they knew her father had stolen a car and robbed a bank? Brandy didn't want to think about it. She was ashamed of her father. As she experienced a more normal life, she found she didn't want to be near him.

Annette fought back her anger. How dare that man refuse to properly feed this baby! "You know, I have some formula that upsets Seth's stomach. You can have it. Maybe it will agree with Ethan." Annette suggested. "Do you want to try?" Annette would willingly to give up some of Seth's formula to make sure Ethan was nourished. She wasn't about to tell Brandy the children were eating the same formula. Annette realized she didn't know the girl well enough to be honest with her.

"That would be really nice. Thank you, mam." Brandy stated. She was very relieved to know she would be able to properly feed Ethan. Brandy liked these people. It felt good to be in a loving household. Something Brandy hadn't experienced since her mother passed away.

"You can call me Annette. I'm not that much older than you are." Annette said with a smile. Brandy made her feel like a middle age woman. "Let's go into the kitchen. The formula is on the top shelf."

The young mothers walked into the kitchen. Annette reached up and pulled the formula from the shelf. She turned the can over to read the mixing instructions. The powder could be mixed a bottle at a time with lukewarm water which would be perfect for Ethan as they traveled. Annette ran some cold water from the tap into a small pitcher. She added the measured amount of formula into the water. After mixing the powdered formula thoroughly, she poured the milk in a clean baby bottle. She heated the bottle in a small saucepan until the formula felt lukewarm when Annette tested it on the inside of her arm. She handed the prepared bottle to Brandy so she could feed Ethan.

Just as Brandy took the bottle from Annette's hand, George came into the kitchen and snatched the baby bottle from Brandy's hand. "What is this crap?" He snapped. "This kid doesn't need any of that fancy for-mula! Dump it out! Now!"

"Mr. Sims!" Annette stated trying to stay calm. It took her full strength and willpower to hold her tongue. "This is formula my son can't drink. It will be far easier on your grandson's stomach than whole milk. It won't cost you anything to let him try." Annette stated with more than a little anger in her voice.

"He can try but I'm not paying for no fancy milk! Got that girl!" He pointed a finger in Brandy's face with fire in his eyes. She looked back down to the floor. Annette could see the disappointment in the young woman's face. Annette felt so sorry for this girl. She wanted to take a baseball bat to George Sims. He was impossible!

Brandy's tears mounted. She tried so hard to take care of Ethan. All she wanted was to be a good mother. The kind of mother she remembered her mother being. She didn't want the baby to be taken away from her. After George stormed out of the room, Annette put a loving arm around Brandy. "It will be alright, sweetie, you'll see. Jesus will help you take care of your son."

Annette allowed Brandy to calm her emotions slightly before she spoke to the girl again. "Where is your mother?" Annette asked. She thought it was odd that this man had custody of these children. He wasn't a proper caregiver for them.

"She died four years ago. I really miss her. Dad drank then but nothing like he does now. It's been really hard." Brandy stated as she released the tears in her eyes.

Annette's heart went out to the girl. She wanted to protect the child and her child.

***

Later, Mary noticed the children went to the small bedroom to get something. From the living room, she heard shouting coming from the small room. The voice of George Sims could clearly be heard. "You are to stay in this room. Hear me? I don't want you talking to those people. Got that?" Mary didn't understand why he was isolating the children. She decided it was best if she went back into the kitchen to help Annette with supper. Whatever it was, it was none of her business.

***

Annette could hear Seth crying in the back bedroom. No doubt the shouting in the other bedroom had awakened him. He needed her attention. The young mother went to the larger bedroom, picked up her son, comforted him, and laid the infant on the changing table next to his bassinette. With his diaper changed, she brought the infant to the kitchen to warm some formula for him. It was time for his supper. She wanted to feed her son before she served supper to everyone else. Seth wasn't very patient when it came to his meals. The adults could wait a half hour or so. Seth couldn't!

Annette pulled baby food jars out of the refrigerator to heat with the prepared baby bottle. After the formula and the 2 jars of baby food were heated, she placed them on the kitchen table along with a baby spoon and Seth's bib. Annette unscrewed the top of the baby bottle as she balanced the infant in her arms. A small amount of formula was poured into the powdered rice cereal. She mixed the cereal and milk to make a runny mixture. Seth knew what was coming. He moved his little arms and legs with excitement sucking his lips together in preparation of his next meal. In short order, Annette placed the small bib on the squirming infant. She held her son in her lap with him resting on her left arm. Her left hand gently around his left arm to keep him from spilling the baby food as she fed him. She would be glad when he was old enough for a highchair. It would make this process much easier. She spooned strained peaches and rice cereal into his little mouth. The baby food was something new to Seth. At 2 months, he just wasn't satisfied on the formula. The doctor suggested giving him some very runny rice cereal and a little bit of fruit a couple of times a day. Sure enough, Seth slept much better and seemed to be a much happier baby. This boy loved his food! The baby sucked the contents in his month with pleasure. Annette gave him some formula from his baby bottle to wash down the excess food. When the baby food was completely eaten, Annette placed the infant carefully on her shoulder. Gently patting his back to relieve any excess gas off of his little stomach. In one smooth, fluid motion, she got up from the table with the infant still on her shoulder. She picked up his baby bottle and walked into the living room where her husband sat talking with the college students.

"Honey, would you please take Seth and finish giving him his bottle while I get the rest of supper ready for everyone else." Annette asked Jay. He reached for his son. Glad to be able to spend some time with the boy for a few minutes.

"Sure honey. I love this time with Seth. It's our bonding time." Jay stated. He noticed the young men in the room seemed embarrassed at the actions of the young father. George walked off in a huff. Evidently, he didn't think a father should feed his baby. Henry, Bill and Mary found the scene touching. They enjoyed watching the unconditional love between young couple. Bill lovingly took his wife's hand to show her loved her too.

Annette walked back into the kitchen. Opening cabinet doors, she pulled out serving bowls of all shapes and sizes. She didn't have enough of one kind to feed everyone so they would just have to eat on mismatched table settings. She pulled spoons from the silverware drawer and placed them in a basket in the center of the table. In another basket, she placed several different kinds of crackers. A plate of sliced cheese was placed next to the basket of crackers. Then paper cups were placed on the end of the kitchen counter along with a pitcher of ice cold water drawn their well.

Realizing what Annette was doing, Mary left the living and walked into the laundry room. In short order, the middle aged woman came out of the laundry room carrying a wicker basket piled with food. She pulled fresh baked bread, plum jelly, and a Tupperware container full of assorted cookies from her basket. She picked the container of cookies back up again and chuckled. "Maybe we should save these for later. We don't need our dessert right now!"

Annette chucked at the sweet woman. "I still have some cookies too, so we are set for desserts. I agree, we can have the desserts later." Stirring the large pot of chili soup a couple of additional times, Annette decided that it was ready to serve.

She walked into the living to announce dinner to her guests. "I think we will have to eat in shifts because I don't have a great deal of table space. I can seat eight in the kitchen at once if two people are willing to sit on opposite corners. Let's have the men come in first. Mr. Hapfield, Mr. Colton, David, Jason, Norman, Jay, and Mr. Sims, would you please come into the kitchen to eat. After you are seated, I will dish out your soup and hand it to you. Mrs. Colton, the children and I will eat in the last shift."

As George walked past Annette to get to his place at the table, he said with a sneer, "Them kids don't need to eat. They ate too much already."

"There is plenty for everyone. No one goes hungry in my house, Mr. Sims. The children will eat with Mrs.

Colton and I." Annette said firmly. God forbid, she was growing to hate this man.

"No, they won't!" he replied. "Those kids are to stay in that room!! Understand me!" He shouted. "Now give me my food!" Annette wanted to deny George his food just like he was denying his children. Only propriety and the presence of the other guests kept her from treating him in such a manner.

***

Each man including George Sims received a piping hot bowl of soup. The bread, lunchmeat, and potato chips, the college students brought were placed in the center of the table. In reality, there was plenty of food for everyone. The Lord had provided well. George managed to get two additional refills of soup. If nothing else, the man could eat. Annette didn't fill the third bowl as fill. The man was making a pig of himself at the expense of his children. There were others to feed. Annette was determined that everyone would get their fair share. The college students, whom she expected to be exorbitant eaters, only took one bowl of chili each. They really enjoyed Mary's homemade bread and plum jelly though.

"This is really good, Annette!" David said. "I wish I had room for more. We stopped at Donald's Drive Inn before we left Chadron, so I wasn't very hunger. We didn't know we would get feed so well. Much better than what we would have eaten on the road or camping tonight. You are an excellent hostess!"

George got up from the table. "Yeah, it was alright. Too much seasoning in the chili though." With that statement, he walked out of the kitchen and into the living room to find a place in the recliner in front of the small bedroom door. Annette realized he was attempting to intimidate whoever went into that room. Mary noticed it, too.

***

After the rest of the men finished eating, Mary Colton walked past Mr. Sims and tapped on the small bedroom door. To her surprise, he didn't say anything to her. Hopefully, he realized he had met his match. She wasn't looking for trouble, but she wasn't taking any guff either.

"Supper is ready. There is room at the table for you. Why don't you come have something to eat with Annette and I?" Mary asked. The woman's tone of voice was soft and welcoming. God gave her a way with children. They knew she loved them as God's creations.

Brandy's head hung to the floor. Rick moved his eyes away from Mary's to the recliner on the opposite side of the door. He noticed his father sitting there. Rick didn't dare move from this room without suffering the consequences. "Dad told us we weren't allowed to go eat in the kitchen. We are to stay right here." Brandy stated a little more loudly than was needed. She wanted to make sure their father could hear her.

"I can bring something to you." Mary suggested. "It won't be any trouble."

"That would make him even madder." Rick stated quietly. The boy didn't want his father to hear his reply. Mary noticed some wrappers from convenience store crackers on the cot next to Rick. Apparently, that had been their supper while George was out in the kitchen gorging himself on hot soup. Rick carefully picked up the wrappers. He wadded them up and placed them in his pants pocket where they couldn't be seen. The boy didn't want his father to know Brandy had brought the food into the farmhouse against their father's orders.

"Alright! I know you have to follow your father's wishes. If he changes his mind, there is plenty of food for everyone." Mary couldn't believe what she had just heard. Her dislike for George Sims had strengthened in multitudes. He was just plain cruel to those precious children. George had a very satisfied look on his face as Mary walked around his recliner and into the kitchen. The Lord and I will have to have a talk about this one, Mary thought. Love Thy Neighbor just became nearly impossible with George Sims as her neighbor.

Mary signaled Annette to follow her to the laundry room. She didn't want anyone to hear what she had to say. Bill was in the laundry room putting away some of his clothing and making up his cot.

"It this a private conversation or can I join in?" He asked in a kidding manner.

"No, you can hear this one." Mary stated. Bill noticed her voice deepening with anger. What set her off, he wondered. He suspected it involved the Sims children.

"That man, if I can even call him that, won't let those children come to the table to eat! I went in to get them. The little girl told me that he told them they weren't allowed at the table. I asked if I could take some food to them. The boy said that would make their father even angrier. I noticed some cracker wrappers on the cot next to the boy. I think they brought the food with them from the car. He has evidently refused to let them eat. He positioned himself in the recliner in front of their door to make sure he was obeyed. I'm so angry, I would like to hang him from the loft pulley on the top peak of the barn." There was steam coming out of Mary's ears. Bill had seen this look before. He knew better than to tangle with his wife when she was in this mood.

"What should we do? I hate to have them sitting in that room with so little food." Annette stated. She was thankful the children had something to eat even if it wasn't very nutritious.

"I don't think we can do anything." Bill stated. He seemed to be the cooler head of the group. "They are his children. We know they eat something tonight even if it wasn't much. I think we should leave it alone for now. You hear me, Mary. Please don't raise a fuss!"

"I don't like it!" Mary was still steaming like a loco-motive ready to explode.

"I know. We will keep an eye on them. Maybe we can sneak something to the children later to give them a snack." Bill suggested.

***

Annette was inexperienced enough she didn't know how to handle this situation. She disliked the idea of the children not having a proper meal. This selfish man had the final say over his children which seemed very wrong.

Annette felt guilty about eating without feeding Brandy and Rick, but she didn't have a choice. The situation made Mary so agitated, she didn't have much of an appetite either. After the women finished eating, they put the extra food in the refrigerator. It didn't take long before the dishes were washed. The kitchen in proper order for breakfast.

Annette walked back into the living room where the men had made themselves to home on the couches. No room at the Inn! She walked back into the kitchen and slide a wooden chair into the living room for additional sitting space. Then she sat down to visit with their guests.

"Do you have any idea how you are going to sleep all of us?" Henry Hapfield asked. He noticed there were more people than beds. There had to be a way to make this work in Henry's estimation, but how?

"I have plenty of camping cots scattered throughout the house. When they are set up, they will keep you up off of the ice cold floors. You can use your blankets, pillows, or sleeping bags on the cots to keep warm. The Sims family will take the smaller bedroom, the Coltons will take the laundry room, and Mr. Hapfield why don't you take one of the recliners. Why don't the three of you boys flip a coin for the other recliner and the couch? The odd man out can take a cot. Jay and I will take our bedroom because we have everything set up for Seth in there. Seth gets up in the night, so I want to be close to him to keep him from waking up the rest of the household. If someone else comes tonight, then we will have to figure out how to place them in the kitchen." Annette instructed. "Any questions?"

"Why do I have to sleep in there with those kids? I want the bed!" George demanded. "I deserve a bed not some stupid camping cot!" George thought his status as a guest gave him special privileges over everyone else. He couldn't see the other side of the situation. George only thought about George!

***

"Mr. Sims, my wife told you how everyone is going to sleep. Please cooperate with her." By the firm tone in Jay's voice, he wasn't playing with this disgusting man. Jay gave Seth back to his mother and stood up to show he meant what he said. Annette walked away to put

Seth down for his evening nap. Jay's body language was enough to intimidate the scruffy man.

***

"Alright, that will work!" George stated as he backed down when he realized Jay would defend his wife. The man was a real bully. Surprisingly, he was smart enough to know when to back down. George decided the farmer was stronger than he looked. A fight with him might not be a good idea! "Got any beer?" George asked in an attempt to change the subject. He craved his beer in the evenings after a large meal. He doubted this so-called Christian family had any alcohol in the house, but it was worth asking.

***

The three students looked at each other. Jason signaled the other boys to come into the kitchen. "What do you think, should we go get the beer from the car?" Jason asked his buddies.

"I sure hate to share with that guy!" Norman stated. The young man disliked very few people, but he disliked Mr. Sims. Somehow, Norman knew who would drink most of the beer. He felt very intimidated by George Sims. The man was frightening to say the least.

"I think we should go get the beer. Maybe it would calm him down. I'm afraid if we don't, he's just going to get meaner and meaner. He may simply go to sleep with a beer or two in him." David advised. He thought they would simply have to get along with this mean spirited man so long as they were snowbound.

"Agreed!" Jason said with the conviction of a wise man. "I don't trust this guy at all. If we can get him to go to sleep maybe the rest of us can sleep more peacefully. Since I bought the beer, I will go out to the snow and get it." This was the first time Jason had ever been put into a position where he had to think about the safety of others. It was a mental rush! Overwhelming really! Jason felt he became a man capable of handling any situation.

"Would you look for the bottle of Schnapps while you are at it?" Norman asked. He thought the bottle was in his pocket when they came into the house, but he couldn't find it anywhere. "I think I dropped it in the snow."

Jason rolled his eyes. So much for manhood! Norman was always losing things. "Ok, Norm, I'll look. As hard as it's snowing and blowing in the dark, it will be like looking for a needle in a haystack. I can try, but that's all I can promise!"

"What?" Norman was totally lost by the expression. He hadn't ever heard the express of "Needle in a Haystack".

"Never mind!" David said. "It's not important."

***

Jason put on his jacket. He wished he had a warmer coat. The wind was intense and pushing on the farmhouse door as Jason opened it. The snow pelted his face. He could barely see the top of David's car through the blowing whiteness. The darkness made things even more difficult. The security lights set on thirty foot poles above the driveway offered only limited illumination. When Jason reached the car, he pulled against the wind to open the back driver's side door. It took all of his strength. He heard popping and cracking from cold metal as he pulled the door further open. His best guess was they had about 15-20 inches of snow. It was level with the upper portion of the wheel wells. With the drifting, it was really hard to tell. If it kept snowing this hard, it would be really deep by morning. Jason's legs were getting tired from trying to walk in the knee high snow. He picked up the case of beer. The young man looked briefly for the bottle of Peppermint Schnapps but didn't see it. The student wasn't going to spend very long looking in this cold and wind. His hands and feet were freezing. His ears and nose felt numb. It was too cold to stay out here very much longer. The Schnapps wasn't that important! He closed the car door leaving blown snow on the inside of the vehicle. It would melt later. In no time, Jason was back to the warm farmhouse.

David and Norman greeted him at the front door. "Did you find it?" Norman asked. Norman was fixated on the bottle of Schnapps even though he really didn't want to drink it.

Jason shook his head in the negative. "It wasn't in the car as far as I could tell in the dark. The wind was blowing so hard I couldn't stay out there very long to look. I knew right where the beer was, so it wasn't a problem to find it." Jason stomped his feet on the doormat to remove the excess snow before coming further into the house. He thought of his mother. She would have a fit if he left wet snow on her carpeting!

"Did I hear someone say "Beer"!" George asked from his recliner. "Can I have some? Where is it? I'm really thirsty!"

"Sure." Jason said as he opened the cardboard box in his hand and removed a can of beer for Sims. Jason passed the can to David and David passed it to George. "Would anyone else like some?" Jason offered as he removed his jacket. He checked to make sure the last of the snow was removed from his boots. The student was so cold, he stood beside the gas stove curling his fingers over each other to warm them. He stomped his feet to get the circulation back into his toes.

Everyone declined accept David and Norman. They wanted at least one beer to prove their manhood. Somehow, they thought they would feel grown up with the beer in their hands. When no one else was drinking, the fun was soon removed from the experience. Norman poured half of his can down the bathroom sink later in the evening.

"I still can't figure out where that bottle of Peppermint Schnapps went. I had it in my pocket when we left the car and I started walking to the farmhouse. I got in the house and looked all through the bedding. I checked my pockets. Nothing! I lost it some place between the car and the house." Norman didn't like to lose things. He didn't think the bottle would fall out of his loose jacket pocket. He didn't know whether he should be angry or curious. He had a mystery on his hands. Maybe it will be solved in the daylight.

"Well, if nothing else, it will be well chilled when Jay finds it in the spring!" David joked.

"I would rather find it now." Norman declared. He didn't like the idea of someone else enjoying it. More importantly, it left something undone. That wasn't Norman's personality. He liked closure.

"So, would I, kid. So, would I!" George piped up. He would try to find that bottle tomorrow before he left with those brats of his. That Schnapps would really taste good on the road, George thought.

***

"I have some cookies and coffee in the kitchen, if anyone is interested." Annette offered. She wanted to offer an alternative to the beer being offered in the living room. She assumed the middle aged crowd would join her.

"That sounds far better to me," Bill stated. "I love sweets after a good meal."

"You love sweets anytime." Mary laughingly stated. She knew her husband well. Bill had had a sweet tooth as long as she had known him.

"You know, those cookies sound pretty good to me too." Henry decided cookies sounded far better than beer. He never was much of a beer man. Plus he knew the company in the kitchen would be more wholesome.

"If it's one of my wife's chocolate chip cookies. I'm in." Jay said as he left his chair racing with the others to the kitchen table. Jay really appreciated Annette's cooking. Annette felt proud of herself. She liked to please her husband.

***

Annette and Jay were exhausted. They decided to get some sleep since Seth would have them up in the middle of the night. "Please make yourselves to home. We will see you in the morning." Jay stated. "If you need anything, please let us know." Annette went off to their bedroom to get settled for the night. It was customary for Jay to walk over to the front door to make sure the door was locked. The young man looked out the window in the door to see how much snow had accumulated.

***

After Mary and Bill finished their cookies and coffee, they arose from their chairs. "I think I will turn in. It's been a long day." Mary declared. She didn't want to go back in the living room where George Sims was reclining. Sims had several beer cans on the end table beside the chair. He was drinking his fill just like he ate.

"I'm right behind you honey. I want to finish the rest of my coffee." Bill stated.

***

"I sure wish I could have gotten to Denver tonight." Henry stated. "Joan's father isn't very good. I'm afraid he will die, and I won't be there to comfort her."

"I understand. Just know that God is with her. He has his arms around her when you can't be there. This storm happened for a reason. You were trapped here for a reason. God has a plan for us as it is stated in Jeremiah 29:11. Everything will be alright!" Bill stated trying to find the right words to comfort Henry. The two men talked until Henry became so tired that he retired to the recliner in the living room while Bill went to join his wife in the laundry room.

As Henry took his recliner and covered himself with a blanket, he noticed George Sims was asleep in the opposite recliner. Sim's mouth hung open. He was gasping for air. He puffed, mumbled, and went back to sleep. Empty beer cans were distributed on the floor. The paper box with the remainder of unopened beer placed beside his chair. It was clear Mr. Sims had taken ownership of the entire case!

The students were watching television. They had set up cots for David and Norman. Jason took the couch because he was the shorter of the three young men. They were nearly asleep. Henry guessed the beer they consumed, and the warm room made them sleepy. The middle aged man pulled his blanket more tightly around himself. He was ready for bed too.

Chapter 9

The Last Rescue

Same Night

Suddenly the car radio squealed, and static could be heard on the other end of the line. Sargent Chad Brown wondered how late it was. The car radio stated it was 9:45. Possibly getting too late to go to the Mills Farm although he knew they were prepared to take in stranded travelers for the entire night. He imagined with the new baby, they were up and down the better part of the night.

"Officer Brown are you there?" A cold chill ran through the officer. He had a feeling this call wasn't going to be good. "This is Ralph James from Wahlstrom Ford's Towing Service. We were calling in response to a car accident in your area, but we can't get there due to the semi accident blocking Highway 385. We are on our way to help with that accident in a few minutes. A farmer in your area said he saw the taillights of a car flashing on and off from a snowbank. Apparently, he was out checking on his cattle in the blowing snow. It seems the car went into a ravine. The farmer didn't think he could get them out without some help, so they called dispatch who called us. The farmer didn't know if anyone in the car was hurt. Can you see if you can locate this vehicle and attend to any passengers? After the roads clear, we will pull the car out of the ditch and bring it back to our impound lot."

"Will do. I think I will stop and pick up Mrs. Mills. She's a nurse and can help me with anyone who is injured." Chad replied hoping that Mrs. Mills would be willing to get out in the cold, but truly thinking that she would. There should be other people at the house to care for the Mills baby. Chad thought Jay would want to come with them. He could sure use Jay's help if anyone was hurt.

***

Jay took one last look outside the window in the front door before he went to bed. He had his hand on the deadbolt ready to lock the door when he noticed car lights in the driveway. It was Sargent Brown's patrol car. Was he bringing additional guests to the house? Everyone was welcome, but they were getting pretty full.

Jay greeted Chad Brown at the door. "Chad, come on in. You must be half frozen." At the sight of the patrolman, George Sims suddenly woke up. In one fluid motion, he got up out of his recliner and walked into the small bedroom. He closed the door behind him. Jay hoped he was going to bed. Maybe Jay would feel more at peace with the man locked away. The young man felt a protective need to watch over the remaining members of the household.

"Jay, I need you and Annette's help. Is she still up?" Chad declared with urgency in his voice. "I was notified about a vehicle that has gone off of the highway a couple of miles south of your house. A farmer reported seeing taillights flashing on and off in a ravine. I don't know if there are injuries. Since Annette is a nurse, I was hoping she could come along to give medical care."

Annette heard the conversation between Jay and Chad Brown from the bedroom. She immediately walked into the living room. "Of course, I will go with you," Annette Mills replied before Officer Brown could even ask her.

"No…you don't!" replied Jay Mills. "You just had a baby remember?"

"Jay, I'm fine. These people need our help." Annette replied. She thought Jay could be so protective at times. Part of her enjoyed that protection. Sometimes it was irritating.

"Then I'm coming with you!" Jay's voice was stern. Annette knew this voice. Clearly, he wouldn't back down.

"Who will keep an eye on Baby Seth?" Annette asked hoping the thought of their son would keep Jay at home.

"I could really use Jay's help too. Is there someone here who can keep an eye on Seth?" Chad asked. If the vehicle had been seriously damaged, Chad would need Jay's strength along with his own to get the passengers out of the car.

Mary Colton heard the front door open. The voices of Jay Mills and Chad Brown drew her to the living room. Her curiosity got the best of her. She walked from the laundry room to the living room dressed in her night clothes. "I will dear! I've been wanting to cuddle that little guy anyway. He will be in good hands. Chances are, he will sleep most of the time you are gone. He's such a good baby! I know you have prepared bottles in the refrigerator if I need them."

***

With that, Annette and Jay left the farmhouse with Officer Brown. Jay knew the landscape. He had a pretty good idea where the car might have gone off of the highway. He pinpointed the possible location in his mind. Then explained the location to the officer. Chad Brown agreed. It didn't take long to locate the taillights of the 1975 Chevy Blazer sticking up out of the snow. Someone was in the car, because the brake lights on the vehicle just flashed. The rescuers hoped they would find the passengers unharmed.

Annette and Jay followed the patrol car in their 1970 Ford F350 Truck with 4 wheel drive. Jay had assembled the vehicle with a front end winch. He thought they could attach the winch to the wrecked vehicle to either salvage it or keep it from going further down into the ravine. When they reached the sight of the accident, Jay noticed the Blazer was sloped with the headlights facing down into the snow. More than half of the car was buried in the frozen mass. It was hard to tell how much damage the car had sustained at this angle. It appeared the vehicle was lodged into the hillside between two fence posts.

Chad positioned the patrol car beside the truck facing the accident. The officer and Jay excited their vehicles to examine the scene of the accident. The officer was very thankful the driver had pressed on his brake lights. In this blowing snow and darkness, they wouldn't have found the car otherwise.

"That car is balanced on an outcropping of sandstone. For now, those fence posts are holding it precariously in place. I don't know how long they can sustain the weight of the vehicle. I suggest we take the winch from the truck and hook it onto the back bumper of the Blazer. It will secure the car as we remove the passengers. We can use the patrol car to transport victims to our house." Jay Mills suggested. "What do you think, Chad?"

"I think that's viable. I would like to tie a rope from the patrol car down to the other car to use as a snow guide. If the visibility gets much worse, we are going to have problems seeing between the vehicles in the dark and blowing snow." Chad suggested. He opened his trunk and pulled out a length of rope and several snow shovels that he thought he would need. "Let's take the rope and winch down to Blazer at the same time. I would feel better if that car was secured before we started moving any passengers to safety."

"So would I!" Jay agreed. "I could try to pull the Blazer out of the ravine after we have the passengers safely out of the way."

"No, I think we should leave the salvage work to Wahlstrom's. Let's just keep this a rescue mission." Chad didn't think it was wise to bring the Blazer out of the ravine. They would end up parking it on the highway for the snowplows to hit later. Plus the officer wasn't sure of the amount of damage the vehicle has sustained. He didn't want to make the damage worse if the car was repairable.

Jay leaned into his truck where Annette was still seated. "Honey, we are going to secure the vehicle in the ravine with the winch from this truck. Chad is taking a rope down to use as a snow guide in the darkness and blowing snow. Please stay here until the damaged car is secured. Agreed?" Jay asked his wife. Annette knew Jay was only thinking of her personal safety.

"OK. I'm going down there after that! We need to take care of those passengers!" Annette's patience was only so thick. She knew the longer the passengers were in the car without heat, the greater the chances they would have frostbite. Let alone any other injuries from the impact!

A long rope was tied to the bumper of the patrol car, then around Officer Brown's waist. He and Jay took the end of the winch with them as they crawled and scooted down the embankment. They had to fight against the winds to keep their balance. Once the winch and rope were secured onto the bumper of the Blazer, the men walked back up the hill to the patrol car for additional equipment. Pulling themselves on the rope the entire way. Jay checked his vehicle to make sure it was firmly parked. He started the winch until it was taunt between the truck and the Blazer.

"Ok, Honey. Let's go get those passengers! Hang onto the rope all the way down the hill to help keep your footing. Jay handed his wife a snow shovel. "This shovel will help to balance you. We will need them in the ravine. Jay and Annette hung onto the rope as they carefully walked down the slope with snow shovels in their opposite hands. Chad carried a crowbar, a flashlight, and a shovel with him from the trunk of his patrol car.

When they reached the outside of the damaged vehicle, Jay checked the structure to be sure the winch was holding. The men started digging around the driver's front door. The snow was about 15 inches deep. It was falling in large flakes and accumulating very quickly. The wind was making visibility more and more precarious.

Chad made sure the car was firmly placed. It won't slip when they were unloading the passengers. He hoped the number of injuries would be minimized. Chad shined his flashlight into the car window to find people moving around inside the car. He could see two adults for sure in the front seats. He thought there might be children in the backseats but couldn't see them for sure.

The men were able to release the front car door by wedging a crowbar between the door and the frame. It took all of Chad and Jay's strength to pry the door open. It was jammed into the frame upon impact. A rush of cold air entered the cab when the door suddenly came open. A man and women huddled together as much as they could in their bucket seats shivering from the sudden blast of extremely cold air.

"Hi folks, I'm Sargent Chad Brown from the Nebraska Highway Patrol and this is Jay and Annette Mills. We are here to rescue you and take you to safety. You will be taken to their farmhouse, a couple of miles away, for food, rest, and medical care."

"I'm Dennis Fairfield, this is my wife, Louise, and our children Mark and Susan. We were on our way back to Chadron from North Platte when this storm hit. I'm sorry to say I ignored the roadblock at Alliance because we had to be back to work in Chadron tomorrow. The roads in Alliance didn't look that bad." Dennis felt he had to express his guilt to the officer. It was the only honest thing to do.

"Will you please take the children first?" Louise requested. She was too cold to care about the small talk. "I'm concerned for their safety." In her opinion, any other issues could be dealt with when everyone was safe and warm.

"Is anyone hurt? We will get you out as soon as we can. I think we can take you all at once. I really need to know if anyone is injured. I would prefer to take the injured people up the hill first." Chad Brown instructed. "Annette, would you please check each passenger?"

***

Annette was suddenly placed in a position of authority she hadn't expected. "Mr. Fairfield what about you? Are you hurt?" Annette asked with the compassion of a nurse on duty. She visually checked him over making sure he didn't have any injuries.

"I have a bump on the head, but I'm fine." stated Dennis Fairfield. Annette changed her position to check the superficial bump on his head. She was satisfied it wasn't serious. "My hands and feet are very cold." Dennis was more concerned about his family. "My wife is shivering. She will be much happier if she knows the children are safe. Please take them to your patrol car first. The children appear to be fine. They have been surrounded by the coats we had in the car." Annette listened to the gentleman but continued her examination.

"Mrs. Fairfield, please tell me about you. Trust me, we will take good care of all of you." Annette commanded. "We just need to make sure we don't have any serious injuries before transporting you to the farmhouse."

"My feet feel very numb and ache really bad. I have been sitting on my hands, so they aren't so bad. Mostly

I'm just very cold." Annette noticed Mrs. Fairfield's voice was weakening as she spoke. The woman was evidently in a great deal of pain.

"Chad, I think we will need to take Mr. Fairfield first because we have to move him to get the others out of the Blazer. Then we should take Mrs. Fairfield. They need to be in the patrol car where it's warm. The children can be carried up by you and Jay after their parents are in the patrol car." Annette stated enjoying the little bit of power she had with the authority she was given and yet fearing the consequences of her actions.

"I agree!" Chad said. "Mr. Fairfield can you walk? If so, I will guide you up the hill. You will need to follow the snow guide I have tied between the cars. Keep a hold on the rope. It is secure enough that you can use it to propel yourself up the hill. The climb is steep, and you are fighting the wind the entire way."

"I think so. My feet feel so really cold, I may need some help." Dr. Fairfield stated. He had never felt this venerable in his life. He hated this helpless feeling. Mentally he was fighting it. Physically he had no choice but to give in.

"I will be with you the entire way to the car. Let's give it a try, shall we?" Chad declared trying to sound as cheerful and encouraging as he could. Within a few minutes, the patrolman had the professor seated in the front seat of the patrol car. "While we are getting the rest of your family, there is coffee in this thermos and here are some paper cups. You can drink it while you are waiting. I will be right back with your wife and children." The officer was more than glad to share his coffee if it would help to save lives.

Chad followed the snow guide back down to the Blazer. As he got closer to the car, he heard Mrs. Fairfield refusing to be the next one up the hill. "No, take the children. I can wait. I have to know they are safe." Chad decided she was getting more and more agitated. If she bounced around too much in the car, she could shift its weight and cause the Blazer to move further down the ravine taking Jay's truck with her. Chad didn't want the car to move from its current position. Giving into the woman's demands seemed the sensible thing to do.

"Please calm down, Mrs. Fairfield. Don't shift around in the car so much." Chad requested trying to calm the injured woman.

Quickly, Annette realized what was wrong. The mother bear was protecting her cubs. "Mrs. Fairfield, I would feel the same way if it was my son being left behind. Since it's only a matter of a few minutes, we can take the children first. I have to tell you I'm concerned about leaving you out in this cold any longer than necessary. I suspect your feet are frostbitten. You need medical attention." Annette truly did understand the other mother's need to ensure the safety of her children before her own safety.

The young nurse turned around to face Chad. "In all reality, the longer we argue about this, the longer we are all exposed to this weather. Chad would you and Jay take the children up to the patrol car next? I will stay with Mrs. Fairfield." Immediately, Mrs. Fairfield began to calm down.

Amazingly, the men carried the children up the steep slope with the strength of several men. Annette was concerned the children weren't wrapped in blankets and had light coats on. They really weren't prepared for this weather. In a matter of minutes, the children were placed in the patrol car beside their father. Chad offered a blanket from the patrol car to keep the three people warmer.

Down the hill, the two men slipped and slide for a fifth time. This time Jay carried Mrs. Fairfield back up the slope following the guide rope. He seated her in the front seat of the patrol car close to the blasting heater where she could get warm. The woman was much happier with her family.

Annette and Chad followed right behind Jay carrying the shovels and remaining equipment. Chad made one last trip back down to the Blazer. He untied the snow guide. As Jay released the tension on the winch, Chad removed the winch hook from the bumper of the Blazer. Chad used the rope to propel himself back up to his car following behind the hook to make sure it didn't catch on anything. Jay pulled the metal cable back up into the winch securing the hook when it returned to the bumper of his truck. Annette crawled back into the truck with her husband. She saw Chad untie the rope from the patrol car. After rolling up the cord, he opened the trunk, placed the rope and snow shovels into the car, and crawled into the front driver's seat. Annette was sure both men were freezing cold. They worked a long time to free the family from their frozen prison.

***

"We will have you transported to the Mill's farm in no time." The officer stated. "A tow truck will come back for your car after the storm subsides. In the darkness and deep snow, I can't tell how much damage the vehicle has sustained. Moving it would be very dangerous at this point." Chad suspected the car wasn't drivable since the car doors were so hard to get open with a crowbar, which usually meant body damage, but he didn't want to concern the injured passengers with that detail right now. Getting them to a warm place was far more important. These folks weren't prepared for the weather. No blankets, no heavy coats, no food, or water. Dodging the roadblock. Chad shook his head. Too many people lost their lives on the plains when they didn't take the winter weather seriously enough. These folks were very lucky. The Lord was watching over them.

***

In less than an hour later, the family were settled into the only bed in the Mills house. As it turned out, Dr. and Mrs. Fairfield had sustained frostbite on their toes and the ends of their fingers. Annette decided the best way to get them warm and keep them off of their feet was to place the couple in the king sized bed with the children snuggled beside them. The family had been in the snowbank for four to five hours until a farmer on his tractor saw their car lights. They were lucky someone saw them in the blowing snow and darkness.

"Officer Brown, why don't you come on into the house with us? I know you have been out in this cold for hours. You must be exhausted. At least, let me refill your thermos and get you something to eat." Annette invited. "That is if I'm not breaking any regulations that is." With a smile she walked away from the officer and her husband to tend to her patients.

"Well, Chad, why don't you come on into the house. Annette is right. You could use some coffee and something to eat." Jay invited with a smile on his face. He could use a sandwich himself. Jay began to notice that his stomach was rumbling. The mention of food always did that to him. He burned an enormous number of calories walking back and forth up and down the steep hill in the deep snow. He really was hungry. Jay knew he would have to eat before bed.

Chad watched as the injured couple settled into the Mills' home. No mention was made of their color on the part of the Mills family. Chad hoped there wouldn't be any trouble from any of the other guests. People were really funny about such things. Would there ever be a time when a person's race went noticed? People would be loved as Jesus loves us. Every life is important from conception to death because God created them. Chad pondered.

"I have the Fairfield family all settled into our bed. They are very comfortable all nested together to keep each other warm. I used towels and a large pan of luke-warm water to warm their feet and hands." Annette stated. "I think Mrs. Fairfield is going to need to see a doctor as soon as we can get them to Chadron. Her frostbite seems to be the worst."

"Chad, it doesn't looks like the college students are going to use that recliner over in the corner in front of the small bedroom. You are welcome to take it and get some rest. I'm sure you are exhausted. As late as it is, you probably aren't even on duty right now." Annette invited. "Let me get you a blanket."

"No need. I have one in the car. I think I will take you up on your offer. I have to go out to the car to inform dispatch where I am. Can I given them your telephone number in case there's an emergency? I'll be right back." Chad stated. Thankful to the young couple that allowed him a place to rest. Chad wondered if he could borrow Jay and Annette's telephone to call his wife in the morning. He didn't want to disturb the household tonight. She already knew he wouldn't be home.

"Sure, give them the number. I think they already have it though because they called me this morning to inform us, we were having guests. Better safe than sorry." Annette stated.

Sargent Brown decided that Jay and Annette were right. He sure could use some sleep, and a break from the weather. At this point, he was stranded at the farmhouse along with the other guests. Maybe he should just settle down to some sleep. It might be hours before the snowplows could clear the road. He was exhausted after the last rescue. His body ached for some much needed sleep.

"Thanks again, Jay. I will be right back." With that statement Chad walked out the front door. Annette made her way to the kitchen. She made sandwiches for Jay and Chad and placed them on the kitchen table. The young woman set up cots for herself and Jay in the corner of the kitchen. She moved Seth's bassinette into the kitchen with them along with some diapers and sleepers. If her little pirate woke in the middle of the night, she wanted him to be close to his main source of entertainment. His bottle!

***

When Chad returned to the house, he found one unused recliner ready to make into his bed. Two of the college students were asleep on cots. The third was asleep on the couch. The first gentleman Chad stopped had the other recliner. He decided a very nice person had left the unused recliner for him.

After he began to get comfortable, he began to think about his day. He realized he hadn't heard the results of his inquiry on Sims from the Captain. He knew there was a story. He could just feel it! He didn't realize how correct he was.

***

A couple of hours later, Chad heard the door to the small bedroom open. The officer opened one eye to see who was close to his chair. A young girl came out of the room carrying an infant. They went into the bathroom closing the door behind them. He heard the refrigerator door open and close. A few minutes later they walked back past Chad into the small bedroom. She left the door open. No doubt the room was cold since the temperature outside was near zero and there wasn't any heat in that room. She evidently wanted to warm the room with the heat from the corner stove. Chad could hear voices. He quietly listened.

"What are you thinking girl? Don't leave that door open! That policeman is just outside of the door. He will see me!" George exclaimed with fear in his voice.

He must know that I stole that car and robbed that bank. He's guarding me. I just know it, George thought. The alcoholic was beginning to panic. His own guilt convicting him. It had been hours since he had a drink. He took a case of beer to the bedroom with him. Where was it? He looked across the room. The empty cans and paper carton were on the floor beside his bed. He needed another drink. That was the only way he could deal with feeling so trapped. So guilty! So appressed by the world. He couldn't let himself feel anything. It was too painful!

"Dad be quiet. You are going to awaken everyone in this house." Brandy ordered. She was afraid if her father was arrested, they would take Ethan from her. Fear gripped her. Her father would get her into even more trouble.

"He knows! I know he knows I stole that car and robbed that bank. He knows!" Panic could be heard in George's voice.

What George didn't realize was that Chad just heard George's confession to stealing the car and bank robbery. Where and when, Chad didn't know. Funny how one's own guilt will convict them! Officer Brown stayed where he was in the chair pretending to be asleep. No sense in tipping his hand tonight. He would call the Captain in the morning. Chad would sleep lightly the remainder of the night. Suddenly, he was back on duty. He had a prisoner to guard!

Chapter 10
The Morning After

Mary Colton arose from her camping cot in the laundry room of the Mills house. Her husband, Bill, was still sound to sleep. He had stayed up an hour or so comforting and visiting with Henry Hapfield. Poor Henry, he was so distraught that he couldn't get to Denver to be with his wife. He had really needed Bill's friendship and prayers.

Mary could hear the boys and George Sims talking in the living room last night. The men couldn't have stayed up too late because KDUH-TV went off of the air after Jerry Dishong gave the 10:00 news and weather. There was some kidding and joking about a bottle of Peppermint Schnapps. One of the boys was frantic, he lost the bottle somewhere between their car and the house in the snow. They finally settled down about 11:00 after talking for an hour or so. The house became quiet after Sargent Brown, Jay, and Annette left to rescue the victims of a car accident.

Mary had offered to care for little Seth while they were gone. Mary had checked on the small tike numerous times. The little guy was sleeping soundly. Mary decided she would get a few winks herself while she had a chance. She suspected Annette would need her help in the morning with a house full of people to feed.

Just as Mary finished dressing and came out of the bathroom near sunrise, she could hear a baby crying in an adjoining room. At first, she thought it was the other baby brought in by the young mother. Then Mary thought she better check and make sure that it wasn't baby Seth who needed some attention. Thinking about it, the women found it odd that she hadn't hear either baby stir for some time. She thought maybe the 4 month old was old enough to sleep through the night. She decided to check on little Seth.

To Mary's surprise, she found four black people huddled into Annette and Jay's king sized bed when she went into their bedroom to retrieve Seth from his crib. Seth wasn't in the room. At first, Mary was alarmed. She had promised to take care of the child. He had disappeared. Mary quietly excited the room. She didn't want to awaken anyone. The middle aged women wondered when the family had been brought into the house. She decided it was the family rescued from the car accident. She felt foolish for disrupting their privacy.

Mary noticed a pretty young girl on the edge of the bed watching her every move. "Good morning, dear,"

Mary said with the love only a grandmother can produce. "I'm Mary Colton, who are you?"

"I'm Susan Fairfield, and this lump of coal is my brother, Mark." Susan stated as she looked at her brother with a scowl on her face. "These are my parents, Dennis and Louise Fairfield."

"When did you come in?" Mary asked.

"We have been here since about 11:30 last night. Officer Brown and Mr. and Mrs. Mills rescued us from the snow. They are nice enough to bring us here to rest and warm up. It was really cold in that car." Susan offered. She seemed like a very nice young lady. Mary smiled at the sleepy girl.

"Go ahead and go back to sleep if you want. We will have breakfast ready for everyone in an hour or so." Mary hoped that was the case. She still wondered where Seth had been taken. Mary walked into the kitchen to find Annette and Jay asleep on old army cots. They had moved Seth's bassinette into the kitchen with them. No doubt so Annette could take care of him through the night.

Seth started to stir. He would be awake soon. It was 5:30, no doubt time for his morning feeding. Mary tried to soothe the tiny baby by rubbing his back, but Seth wanted two things and two things only. His mama and his breakfast. Mary lifted the infant from his bed. She thought she would try to find Seth's baby bottle. She didn't know what else to offer the starving child, but the bottle would do for now. First, she would change Seth's soggy diaper. As soon as she unpinned his wet diaper, the cold air from the room hit his little bottom. Seth let out a blood curdling scream of shock and surprise. The cold air wasn't what he was expecting. The scream wasn't what Mary expected either.

Annette was exhausted after being out in the snow so late. She rolled over on the narrow cot. At first, she couldn't figure out why Seth was crying so loudly or why she was sleeping in the kitchen. Her mind raced back to the present. She saw Mary diapering her son.

"Thank you, Mary, for tending to him. I will get up to get his breakfast. No doubt that scream will have the rest of the household up very soon." Annette smiled at the older women who had been so much help through the last 24 hours.

"Let me get breakfast started while you attend to this little guy. I noticed bacon and eggs in the refrigerator. Would you like me to start them?" Mary Colton offered as she handed angry little Seth over to his mother.

"That would be wonderful. I have the ingredients for pancakes too. As soon as I finish with this guy, I will be in to help you." Annette hated to leave the work to Mary, but Seth came first.

"I see you have four more house guests. What happened to them? Was anyone hurt in the accident?" Mary asked.

"Their car went off of the road into a ravine. We had to dig them out of the snow. Chad and Jay had to pry their car door open with a crowbar. Professor and Mrs.

Fairfield are both suffering from frostbite. We needed to get them as warm as possible, so our bed was the best place for them. I don't think the frostbite is too bad for him, but it is for her. We needed to thaw his fingers and toes slowly. She needed the same treatment for her badly frosted feet. She wore flat soled slip-ons without any socks which wasn't enough protection from the bitter cold." Annette stated. "We will need to get her into town see a doctor as soon as the roads clear."

In short order, Annette rose and dressed. She prepared Seth's bottle from the contents in the refrigerator. The infant watched her every move with interest. "This guy is very demanding when it comes to his food. Eating is serious business to him." Annette laughed. She knew her son was just like his father in that regard. Food was very important to both of them.

"I'm glad I can help out," Mary Colton stated as she reached into the lower cabinet to retrieve a skillet. She removed bacon and eggs from the refrigerator. The skillet was placed on the stove. The burner was light with a match from the match holder on the wall. Annette had a gas stove that had to be light manually.

Annette placed water and coffee grounds in a large 12 cup coffee pot the night before. As Seth's formula warmed in a pan of water on the stove, she plugged the coffee maker cord into an electrical socket to get it started. She wanted to be sure she could fill Officer Brown's thermos before he left the house that morning.

He had given up his thermos of coffee to the Fairfields the night before to keep them warm.

The young women turned on the radio to KLRC, the only radio station in the area, to get the latest news and farm reports. Maybe the noise would calm Seth if she replicated their morning routine a little. The young mother pulled a jar for baby food and some rice cereal from the cabinet for the rest of Seth's breakfast.

She remembered she had some canned peaches in the root cellar under the wellhouse which would work nicely for everyone else's breakfast. Maybe she could get her husband to go get them. She hated to ask. He had been out in the cold weather most of yesterday. Thanks to his noisy son, the young farmer was lying on his cot wide awake.

"What can I do to help your girls?" Jay asked lovingly. He knew his wife needed his help this morning with so many people in the house. Jay had livestock to check and feed. He really needed to get up. It took a great deal of effort to make his tired body move.

"Would you go down to the root cellar and get some jars of canned peaches? They will go nicely with our breakfast." Annette asked with a loving smile.

"Sure! Please give me a few minutes to put some pants on." Jay declared. "It's cold in that well house!" Mary turned away from the couple to allow Jay some privacy to dress.

***

Sargent Brown were abruptly awakened by Seth's outburst. Jay walked through the living room to get his winter coat out of the hall closet before he went to the wellhouse. He looked out the window in the front door. He and Chad Brown observed the blankets of snow that covered the yard.

"Chad, do you think the highway will be opened up soon? Nothing is moving out there. You can't even see our tracks from last night. I would estimate the snow to be at least three foot in spots. With the blowing and drifting, it's hard to tell." Jay stated as he put on his heavy winter coat and snow boots. "Your car is buried with the rest of them."

"I agree, Jay. It's really deep in several places. It will take the snowplows some time to get through the massive drifts. I haven't talked with dispatch since last night because I haven't gotten into my car. I don't know how they are coming with the removal of the semitrailer below the Job Corp. I should go check with them before too long. I will need to dig my car out of its drift. Do you have an extra shovel I can borrow? Mine is buried with the car."

"Sure. I'll come out and help you," Jay declared. "Just let me get some peaches from the root cellar under the wellhouse for Annette. Our breakfast awaits!"

"If I know my wife, she has hot coffee ready for you." Jay proudly stated. With those words, Annette came out of the kitchen.

"Daddy, if you will burp your son and finish feeding him his bottle, I will help Mary with breakfast." Annette asked.

"I haven't made it to the root cellar yet." Jay stated feeling torn in several directions at once. "I will be right back. Chad needs to get into his car to radio his office. There's so much snow piled against the patrol car he's going to need some help. Chad, I will be right with you. You can find the snow shovels in the tool shed to the left of the door. Help yourself."

"Ok. I will go on outside and get started." Chad stated. "I need to contact dispatch as soon as possible." Chad wanted to confidently talk to Captain Jacobson about what had become the Sims case. Jacobson needed to know what Chad had heard the previous night. The officer wondered if his captain had gotten any word from the State of Kentucky.

***

Bill Colton stood behind Annette when she talked to Jay. He reached out his firm farmer's hands to the infant. "Let me take this guy, if he will come to me. I can find a corner in the kitchen and feed him while you work. I've had great deal of experience with this job assignment. All we require is a cup of coffee and a baby bottle."

Annette smiled. She liked Bill and thought Seth would too. Baby and bottle were handed off to him.

Seth's eyes studied the man before him. With his bottle in his mouth, the child was content. The stranger offered the right incentive as far as Seth was concerned.

"Mind if I join you," Henry asked with a teasing smile. "I could use some of that black formula over there myself! He sure looks satisfied." Pointing to Seth.

"I hoped you would. Yes, he doesn't seem to mind who feeds him, so long as he's fed." Both men chuckled.

***

Annette began mixing the ingredients for pancake batter into a large bowl. She heated the grill. Mary had bacon started in a skillet. The smell of cooking food waffled into the remainder of the little house. David, Jason, and Norman were the next ones to wander into the kitchen. They took their seats beside Henry and Bill. Waiting for their share of the black formula!

After placing the pancake batter into the hot skillet to form round circles. Annette allowed them to cook. While they were cooking, she placed paper plates and plastic silverware in the table. Syrup, butter, peanut butter, honey, and jelly were added to the tabletop. With cups and glasses above the coffee pot in the cabinet, people could help themselves to their drinking materials. The pancakes were turned over and allowed to finish cooking on the opposite side. When they were ready, Annette placed the completed pancakes on a large platter. More pancake batter was added to the skillet. The hot pancakes were placed on the table for consumption.

***

In the meantime, Mary had fried several pounds of bacon slices to a crispy golden color. She drained off part of the excess grease from the fried bacon. The woman broke several eggs individually into the remaining hot grease. When the eggs were white on the back side, she turned them over to cook the front side of each egg. The bacon and eggs were placed in the middle of the table for the hungry men. The women weren't sure which man was eating more but they were enjoying the hardy breakfast.

By the time Jay and Chad freed Chad's patrol car from its frozen prison, they were ready for breakfast. Stomping snow from their feet and removing their coats, they joined the rest of the men at the kitchen table. "I thought after breakfast, we would try to dig my tractor and snowblade out of the machine shed. We will have to shovel around the wide doors to remove the equipment. If we get the tractor and snowblade out, we won't have to shovel as much snow by hand down the driveway. I thought we could free the cars in the driveway. When the snowplow comes through, we only have to remove the snow that they throw back on us from the highway. If we shovel the far end of driveway now, we will just have to shovel it again after the snowplow passes. We can save ourselves some back breaking work by working this end of driveway first." Jay suggested as he shoved another bit of pancakes into his already full month. He was familiar with this routine. He had it down pat! "Honey, do you have any more of these pancakes? They are really taste good to me this morning!"

Annette smiled as she placed another plate of hot pancakes on the table. "Anyone else need more, there's plenty and more to come." Annette picked up sleeping Seth from Bill's wide shoulder. The infant was sound to sleep. Ready for his morning nap. Bill was experienced with that procedure, Annette thought. Seth was certainly satisfied! She really appreciated the farmer's willingness to help.

Annette placed Seth in his bassinette. She decided it needed to be out of the way, so she picked it up and moved the portable crib to the living room near the heating shove. "How is everyone in here? Would anyone like some breakfast?" She asked as she popped her head into the large bedroom doorway where the Fairfield family had been sleeping. "Some of the men have left the table so there's room in the kitchen to join us." Annette invited. "There's plenty for everyone."

"Can I, Papa?" Twelve year old Mark asked. "I'm starved. Susan, do you want to come with me?"

"You are all welcome. Dr. Fairfield do you and your wife feel like walking into the kitchen? I would be happy to bring your breakfast to you if you don't feel like it." Annette asked.

"Yes, Mark, you and Susan can go get your breakfast. I think I can walk just fine. What about you dear? How are your feet feeling?" Dennis asked.

Annette examined the woman's feet. They didn't look very good. The skin looked red and raw. She knew Mrs. Fairfield would need to be taken to the Medical Clinic in Chadron before 5:00 today or the Chadron Community Hospital Emergency room after 5:00. Annette began to silently pray the roads would clear sooner rather than later.

"I think I can walk." Louise Fairfield stated with a grimace on her face. It was clear to Annette the woman was trying to hide her pain. She didn't want to scare her family. Louise was scared enough for all of them.

"Why don't you sit still?" Annette suggested trying to give the woman a way out of an awkward situation. "I don't think it's a wise idea for you to walk on those feet any more than you have to. I will be back in a couple of minutes with your breakfast. Will bacon, eggs, and pancakes be alright? What do you like on your pancakes?"

"I think you are right. I didn't want Dennis and the children to know just how bad my feet really feel. Bacon, eggs, and pancakes would taste really good. I like butter and syrup on my pancakes." Louise stated with a grateful smile.

"Would you like some coffee? Cream or sugar?" Annette asked.

"Black coffee would hit the spot."

"Then I will be back with your breakfast in a few minutes."

***

Dennis Fairfield entered the kitchen door with his children close behind him. He wanted to chuckle at the surprised looks on the faces of David Abrams, Jason Lee, and Norman Gray. He recognized the boys from his history classes. David had one of his classes now and wasn't doing well.

"Hello, boys," the Professor stated with a serious look on his face. "Imagine meeting you here."

"I'm sorry I skipped your class yesterday, sir." David stuttered with guilt written on his face. "I wasn't feeling well."

"I'm sorry to hear that Mr. Abrams. If you would have attended class, you would have known that I placed your assignments on my office door, because I had to take my daughter to North Platte. Please check with me on Monday for that assignment. We need to have a little talk." Dr. Fairfield announced. He could see the fear in the boy's face. He had sufficiently intimidated the young man. Dennis didn't really want to deal with this issue in front of so many witnesses.

"I'd be there if I were you!" Mark stated in an all knowing voice. "Being in trouble with Dad isn't a good thing. Trust me!"

Everyone at the table chuckled. The tension was eased for everyone but David Abrams. The students left the table with Bill Colton and Jay Mills. They gathered up snow shovels to see if they could open up the machine shed. A relieved David left the room. Working outside would ease the tensions he felt.

Annette assembled Mrs. Fairfield's breakfast on a bamboo serving tray. "I'm going to take this food into your wife, Dr. Fairfield. Do you see anything I may have missed?"

"I don't think so. This food looks really good, Mrs. Mills. It's so good of you to take such good care of us. It's really something to get treated to an old fashioned country breakfast on a Nebraska farm. I wouldn't have experienced this kind of treatment when we lived in Mississippi." Dr. Fairfield stated as the first bites of pancakes entered his mouth.

"Thank you, Dr. Fairfield. We are happy to have you in our home." Annette smiled as she turned to flip another batch of pancakes on the grill before she left the room. "Mark and Susan, are you getting enough to eat?"

"Yes, this is so delicious." Mark smiled at the young women as she left the room with the breakfast tray for their mother.

"Hey, Dad, try this!" Mark exclaimed. "I put peanut butter on my pancakes and then maple syrup! It's great! I've never had that before. Do you think Mom would fix pancakes this way for us at home?"

"You will have to ask your mother." Dennis stated. He learned a long time ago to never speak for Louise. She may not agree with the practice.

"It's really good, Dad. I like it too." Susan stated as she dipped a knife into the peanut butter jar. Spreading the peanut butter over her pancake, she poured on the maple syrup. It smelled really good to Dennis. "Let me try that. Dennis reached for a pancake, the peanut butter, and syrup."

"You are right. This is good. I like it too." Dennis piped up as if he had to defend his children's new menu choice. "We will have to talk to your mother about this."

"Speaking of your mother, children." Annette cheerfully stated when she returned to the kitchen. "She said she wanted you to go see her when you finished eating. I think she wanted a report on your breakfast."

"Is there anything I can do to help you, Mrs. Mills? I would like to go outside and help the other men. Does your husband happen to have some size 13 work boots I could borrow?" Dennis asked.

"Jay wears size 10. I'm not sure we have anything that large. Feel free to look in the bottom of the hall closet to see if you can find anything that will fit you. One thing though…be sure your feet are warm. You have a slight case of frostbite. You don't want to make it worse." Annette advised.

"I have a better idea. Would you mind if I washed the breakfast dishes? With so many people to feed, I'm sure they have added up." Dennis asked. "I worked my way through college washing dishes in a restaurant in Mississippi. I don't think I've forgotten how. Please let me help you, since you have been so good to us!"

Annette smiled. She was thankful for another pair of hands willing to help. She returned to the bedroom to retrieve the empty breakfast tray from Louise Fairfield who had been listening to the conversation in the living room.

"Your husband is a remarkable man. I really appreciate his offer to help with the dishes. That was really nice of him." Annette smiled as Louise handed the bamboo tray to her. "Are you feeling better?"

"My feet are burning like fire. They ache and tingle. The muscles are stiff." Louise complained. "I'm glad Dennis pitched in to help you. I feel guilty that I can't do it."

"Please don't feel that way. Your health is far more important. I just graduated from Nursing School in Alliance. From what I know about frostbite, you should see a doctor as soon as we can get you into Chadron. Staying off of those feet is very important. So for now, just rest. Do you need anything else? I hate to rush away, but I have the last of the pancakes on the grill. I told your children to come see you when they are finished eating." Annette stated. She hated to leave the woman alone in the bedroom, but she didn't have a choice. Annette would have loved to sit and talk with the pretty black woman a little longer.

"That would be wonderful. Thank you so much Annette for your care." Louise smiled. She knew the young woman had her hands full.

***

As Annette left the back bedroom, Henry Hapfield asked to use to telephone to call his wife. He wanted to reach her before she left for the Mile High Hospital in Denver. Henry picked up the telephone receiver to make his call. The voice of a woman called Gladys by the other person on the telephone declared the events of snowstorm to Sofia. It seemed Gladys' husband, Carl, saw the flashing lights of a State Patrol car on the highway. Gladys begins to complain about the State Patrol and how she thinks they should do their jobs. Henry decides to clear his throat in hopes of clearing the second party telephone line.

"Sofia, I think we have someone listening to us," Gladys stated in the middle of her state patrol story. "People are so rude sometimes. They like to tie up the telephone line for hours. You would think they would have some courtesy!"

Henry had enough! "Ladies, I'm sorry to interrupt you, but I need to reach my wife. This is an emergency. Would you please hang up the telephone so I can make my call to Denver? I'm a houseguest on the Mills Farm. This is important!" Henry stated attempting to sound as

162

pleasant as he could behind his growing impatience. "I won't be too long. I promise!"

"I hope not!!" One of the women replied. Two clinks could be heard on the other end of the telephone, then no sounds at all.

Henry checked the telephone number from piece of paper in his wallet. He dialed the telephone numbers using the rotary dial. One number at a time. When he reached the long distance operator, he ordered his collect call to his wife at his father-in-law's home.

"Yes, Operator, I will accept this collect call," Henry heard Joan say on the opposite end of the line.

"Hi, honey. How are you doing?" Henry asks his wife. "How is Paul doing?"

"Not good, I'm afraid. Lisa and Bobby are here now. Bobby got some time off from work. He took the kids out of school. They are eating breakfast right now. Dad is hanging on. I think he's getting weaker by the hour. I'm really worried about him. How about you? Are you still at the farmhouse?" Joan asked her husband as she fought back her tears. She felt an overwhelming need to have him near her.

"Yes, I'm afraid so. I'm going outside with the other men to try to dig the cars out of the snow. I would guess there is 24 plus inches of snow. It's hard to tell. The snow has drifted almost to the bottom of the loft door on Mr. Mills' very large red barn. It would be easy to walk upon the drift and enter the loft. Incredible really! We have a highway patrolman stranded here with us. He's checking right now with dispatch to see how much longer it will be until the snowplows can come through. To make matters worse, a semitruck jackknifed across the highway between here and Chadron just north of the Job Corp, so I can't go back into Chadron either. I will know more after the patrolman completes his call. I'm hoping we can get out later today. If so, I will head on to Denver. Since you will be at the hospital, I won't try to call you unless there is a problem." Henry excitedly spouted out his words. He was so happy to be able to talk to his wife. "I've really missed you! I'm sorry I haven't been there for you! I tried!"

"I know dear, you couldn't help a sudden snowstorm. Getting stranded wasn't your idea either. I hope they get you out of that snow drift pretty soon." Joan tearfully stated. "I love you!"

"At least, I have a safe, warm place to wait. The people who live here are very nice. I miss you so much! I love you, too, honey! I will see you as soon as I can." Henry placed the telephone handle back into its cradle. He stared at the yellow rectangular box on the wall fighting back his own tears. He wanted to be in Denver with Joan right now. For no other reason, than to hold her. After reassembling his emotions, Henry found a heavier coat in Jay's closet, put it over his shoulders, and walked out the front door to join the rest of the men. He could see there was lots of work to be done.

***

The door to the small bedroom opened quietly. One lone face peeked outside of the door. Good, he's gone, George thought. The patrolman had left the recliner and didn't appear to be anywhere in the living room. George walked through the living room listening to the voices of the women in the kitchen. He could only hear one male voice. George peeked out of the glass in the front door of the farmhouse. Against the brightly shining snow, he could see Officer Brown working with Jay Mills to free the patrol car from the snow. George decided, since the officer was outside, it was safe to go into the kitchen for breakfast. He planned to stay clear of Officer Brown as much as possible.

"Well, aren't we a cozy group!" George Sims sneered sarcastically as he entered the kitchen. "No one asked me to breakfast." His body odor destroying the smell of the food. He looked right at Professor Fairfield who was working on a large stack of dirty dishes in the kitchen sink, and said, "What are you doing here?"

The racial dig was very apparent to Annette. She held her tongue but wanted to throw the nasty man in the nearest snowbank. Mary Colton glared. Her anger was written all over her face. Mary still hadn't forgiven George for refusing to feed his children the previous night.

"These lovely people came in late last night. They are stranded in the snow just like you are. Dr. Fairfield was gracious enough to help with the dishes. I'm really thankful to those who have pitched in to make their stay a more pleasant experience for everyone. Your bedroom door was closed this morning, so I assumed you were asleep and didn't want to be disturbed. Where are your children? I would like to feed them some breakfast." Annette stated trying to be as pleasant as she could muster. It was apparent to Mary that Annette didn't like this man either.

"Doctor! Sure! Of what?" George sneered.

"Dr. Fairfield teaches history at Chadron State College." Annette proudly stated.

"Oh! Educated! It's that nice!" George gritted his teeth. He didn't like the idea of an educated negro. George thought a college education was a waste of time.

Annette had no patience with this man's ignorance and bigotry. "What about your children, Mr. Sims?" Annette inquired for the second time. Her voice sounding more irritated.

"Those brats will eat when they are ready," George didn't seem to care if the children were fed or not. "I'm not going to call them!"

"Annette, I will go get them. I'm sure they are hungry." Mary said as she walked into the living room, then through the connecting door to the spare bedroom.

"Children, Annette has breakfast ready for you. Would you like some pancakes, eggs, bacon, and peaches? They are really good! She's a fine cook." Mary noticed the fear on the children's faces. "Come on now. No one is going to hurt you."

Slowly, Brandy and Rick left the bedroom turning their heads from side to side as if inspecting the rest of the house. Brandy protectively held Ethan as if she was afraid someone was going to take him away her. Mary had no way of knowing that the presence of the highway patrolman had frightened them. Nor did she know why.

By the time Mary returned to the table with the children, George had consumed the entire stack of the pancakes, bacon, and eggs that were in the middle of the table. He didn't seem to care that his children hadn't eaten yet. Just so long as he had his fill.

Annette mixed up another batch of pancake batter. She placed more bacon and eggs on the skillet. The canned peaches were completely gone, but she had a few apples in the refrigerator the children could eat. As she assembled the food for the older children, she realized that baby Ethan hadn't had any breakfast either.

"Brandy, does Ethan eat baby food? If so, what kind does he like?" Annette inquired. "I think I have another can of formula you can have. It doesn't settle well on Seth's stomach, so you are welcome to it, if it works for Ethan." Annette was concerned about the child. He was supposed to be 4 months old, but he looked to be about the same size as Seth. She wondered if Brandy gave the infant the care he needed. By the looks of Brandy and Rick, they could use some care themselves.

"No, mam. I haven't started him on baby food yet. I haven't been able to afford it." Brandy replied looking over at her father in the corner of the room.

"That kid don't needs no fancy baby food. He's just fine drinking milk," George growled. He looked over at Brandy. "You hear me girl!" With that statement he stormed out of the room to the relief of everyone around the table.

"What a wicked man!" Mary stated and then didn't say more when she realized her audience was his children.

"That's what our social worker at Children's Services said about him," Rick added. "They don't like each other at all!" Brandy jabbed her brother in the ribs to signal him to silence. Mary guessed there was far more to that story.

"Children's Services?" Mary asked. "Were you in their custody?"

Brandy was suddenly very quiet for several minutes. Mary waited for the child to be ready to speak. "The truth is, we were in protective custody. We aren't supposed to be around him. They placed us in a foster home in Frankfurt. Rick didn't like it there and neither did I. When they threatened to take Ethan from me, we ran away. The only place we knew to go was back to Dad's place."

"Why did you go back to your father?" Mary asked.

Brandy looked to the floor. Very quietly she stated innocently, "I thought Ethan had a right to know his father."

"You mean...is his father." Brandy shook her head in the affirmative. Mary and Annette looked at each other in horror.

Chapter 11
The Departure

⚘

Annette and Mary understood the meaning of Brandy's statement immediately. Dennis was thankful his children were in the bedroom visiting with their mother. Keeping his hands in the dishwater, he shook his head. He had heard some pretty sad stories in his life, but this was one took the cake. Annette realized she had tears running down her face. Just as protectively, she went into the living room to check on her son. Suddenly, she wanted to protect him from that awful man. Mary had heard these stories before when she worked in Lincoln for the Nebraska Children's Services. These children had to be removed from this man. The sooner the better. Mary decided she needed to report this situation immediately.

***

It was still cloudy outside. More snow fell in gentle flakes. The men finished cleaning the snow away from the patrol car. Mary watched Officer Brown crawl inside. The officer started the engine to allow the car to warm. Exhaust escaped from the rear and floated into the dry Nebraska air. Then drifted away from the farm. The rest of the men continued to shovel snow away from the next vehicle.

Sargent Brown radioed the Chadron office. To his surprise, the dispatcher responded immediately. "Jennings, is the Captain in?" Chad asked. "I need to talk to him immediately. Any word on clearing Highway 385? We have 14 people stranded up here at the Mills Farm. At this point, I'm as stranded as they are. We are digging ourselves out, but we need the plows to clear the highway."

"No word yet, Chad." Frank Jennings replied. He was all business on the radio. "You need to let the Captain explain. I will warn you. He's like an old bear this morning. Lack of sleep I suspect. We have had a busy night. I will patch you through!"

"I understand that one! Thanks, Frank!"

"Jacobson, here." Frank was right, the Captain did sound like a bear this morning, Chad thought. The previous night was definitely a rough one.

"Good morning, Captain. Sargent Brown here. I'm still stranded at the Mills Farm with 14 other people. I fished the last family out of a ditch about 11:00 last night. Everyone is doing fine. It could have been much worse. One woman has frostbite on her feet. She will need medical care as soon as we can get her to Chadron.

I think their car is a total loss. Wahlstrom's agreed to come get the car when they can get up here with the tow truck. I know I will have to bring the family back to Chadron. Any luck getting the Safeway semi-tractor trailer off of the road yet? We are getting a second wave of snow. I hope this one doesn't last too long."

"Yes, they have removed the semi. They are now working to remove the cargo that was in the trailer. It shouldn't be long until the highway is clear. Maybe an hour or so. No doubt in my mind, we will be cleaning canned goods from the ditches into mid-summer. I'm told it was quite an ordeal. Additional snow won't help the clean-up, that's for sure."

"I know, I had a witness tell me, the trailer looked like a beached whale laying on its side in the middle of the highway." Chad chuckled at the memory of Norman's statement.

Jacobson laughed. "I think that about sums it up!"

"Any word on that license plate I asked you to run from Kentucky. The suspect is still stranded here at the Mills Farm. I have reason to believe he stole a car and robbed a bank recently. I overhead him admit the crimes to his daughter. I just don't know where and when." Chad explained.

"Yes. As a matter of fact, I just received a telephone call from the Kentucky State Police. It seems Mr. George Sims has been a very busy man. In the span of one day, he stole a car belonging to Helen and Arnold Winford of Frankfurt, Kentucky, and robbed a bank on the outskirts of Frankfurt. To make matters worse, he stole his children who are legally wards of the State of Kentucky. He endangered their welfare when he had them in the car at the time of the robbery."

"I got a real chuckle out of this part. He apparently robbed the bank using his finger in his sweater to look like a gun. The cameras show him removing his hand from his sweater pocket. The teller had a sack of counterfeit bills under her counter they use for training purposes. She put the stack into a paper bag and gave the sack to Sims. He was in such as hurry, that he didn't even realize what she had done. I don't think he caught on because he passed those bills in St. Louis, Kansas City, and Lincoln. He left us a paper trail. Literally! Now that he traveled across state lines, he's wanted for kidnapping and passing counterfeit bills. One other thing…he is suspected of being the father his daughter's baby. This guy is a real winner!" Jacobson said with disgust in his voice. "You need to arrest him as soon as you can. Take him into the Chadron City Jail for processing. We will no doubt extradite him back to Kentucky."

"I didn't think Sims had that much energy. I think he maybe an alcoholic. He can sure put away the beer. How do you want me to handle the situation with the children?" Chad asked. He always hates these cases where he had to separate the children from their parents.

"I will notify the Nebraska Protective Services that you will be bringing the children into them. You can leave the children with the Mills family while you make a trip to Chadron with Sims. You may have to have Mr. Mills bring the injured women to the hospital, if he can get a vehicle out of the driveway. I will see you later, Brown." It was clear to anyone watching from the window of the house, that Chad Brown wasn't happy about the conversation he had on his radio.

"Thanks, Captain." With that statement, the radio went dead. What a mess! Sargent Brown noticed Bill Colton and Henry Hapfield in their advanced years out shoveling the snow away from the cars. They were willing to help dig everyone else out of the Mills driveway. George Sims should be outside helping. The stolen car will be freed from the snow, swiped for evidence, and later returned to the Winford's. Suddenly, Chad found himself determined to make Mr. Sims earn his keep. He wouldn't arrest him just yet. He would get some work out of him first.

Sargent Brown walked back into the house. He was cold and needed sometime to collect his thoughts. He poured himself a cup of coffee, sat down at the kitchen table, and started to empty the cup. Just about that time, George Sims walked into the kitchen. He opened the refrigerator door to look for something unaware that Officer Brown was sitting at the back of the kitchen table. Sims slammed the refrigerator door in anger when the object he sought wasn't available.

"Are you looking for something, Sims?" Chad asked. At the sound of Officer Brown's voice, George jumped a foot into the air.

"Yeah! Some beer! Some place this is! No beer, only one TV channel and one radio channel. What's a person supposed to do around here for fun?" George stated in his booming voice. Chad could hear frustration and anger with each of his words.

"I think it's called work!" Chad replied. "Get your coat on. You can come with me to shovel snow. We have a lot of cars to free before the snowplows get here." Chad was determined to get some work out of this man one way or the other.

"If they get here!" George snapped. "Why should I go out and work in that stuff? It's starting to snow again. Their efforts will be worthless." Then he realized, that if he went outside to help with the snow removed, maybe he could locate the bottle of Peppermint Schnapps the college kid lost in the snow the night before. He could sure use a drink right now.

"Oh, the plows should be here in an hour or so. Now get your coat. This little snow shower won't last very long." Chad waited for an addition argument. George didn't offer one. Instead, he found a jacket of sorts and started out the front door with Officer Brown close behind. Chad wondered if Sims had an ulterior motive. It was apparent, the man didn't want to argue with the state patrolman.

"Did you mean what you said about the snowplows?" Annette asked as she entered the kitchen.

"I sure did! I was headed out to tell Jay. Spread the word, will you? Even though it's getting late, some people will be able to leave here in a few hours. The Captain said the roads in Box Butte County are clear. They are working on Dawes county now. It really won't be long. It took several hours to clear the semi off of the highway. I suspect, the debris will be visible through the mid-summer months. Maybe a Scouting group will come out and clean it up for their community service project." Pointing his head to George, Chad stated, "He's going outside with me." He could see the relief on Annette's face. That man made everyone nervous.

"Thank you, Chad. He's a scary one! I really don't dislike anyone but he's creepy."

"I know. There's a long story associated with him. I'll tell you what I can later."

***

Mary and Annette could see that George wasn't working very hard when Chad wasn't standing over him. No surprise there. George seemed very interested in the car belonging to David Abrams. Mary wondered why the fascination with David's car. She hoped David had removed his keys from the car.

***

The second wave of snow ended almost as fast as it started. The men kept working to free their cars. Every half hour or so they came back into the house to warm themselves with heat and coffee.

Less than an hour later, the women noticed flying snow over the tops of the cars. The sound of trucks shook the little house. Everyone cheered. The snowplows had come at last. The plow could only shovel one lane at a time. He was going south. He would work his way to the Box Butte County line, turn around, and come back north again. Not long after the first plow came through, a second plow could be seen turning onto Table Road. He would clear the unpaved county roads for the farmers living in the area.

The men worked even harder after the snowplow came through the first time. The large blade threw snow from the highway back up into the Mills driveway. Jay had explained this process at breakfast, so no one was discouraged by the additional snow to remove. The first car to be completely freed was the patrol car. It was the last vehicle parked in the driveway and was blocking the other cars. They really needed to get it moved before the snowplow came back. The car would be an obstacle parked part way on the highway asphalt. It could be damaged or pushed up into other vehicles.

"Sims, I need to talk to you." Chad Brown stated pulling his car keys out of his pocket. Suddenly, he was all business. The patrolman was back on duty.

George Sims slowly found his way from the side of David Abram's car to Chad Brown. The patrolman was aggravated by the slowness in the man's steps.

When it didn't fit his agenda, Sims was in no hurry to get anywhere.

"George Sims, I'm arresting you for the robbery of the Frankfurt Bank and for stealing the Ford parked in this driveway. For those charges, you are wanted in the State of Kentucky. You are also wanted for passing counterfeit bills in the States of Kentucky, Missouri, and Nebraska. It seems the bills the teller in the Frankfurt bank gave you were counterfeit bills used for a training exercises. Since they were passed in three different states, you are wanted for counterfeiting across state lines which is a federal offense. Speaking of state lines. Since the children are wards of the State of Kentucky and you took them out of the state, there may be kidnapping charges. You will be taken to Chadron until you can be extradited to Kentucky." Brown stated. The patrolman read the Miranda Rights to George Sims and arrested him.

"Which one of those kids ratted on me?" George asked with vehemence in his voice. "I didn't know those bills were counterfeit. I swear I didn't."

"None of the children said anything." Chad stated shaking his head. The man just couldn't admit he was to blame for his own actions. "You ratted on yourself when you panicked while I was resting in the recliner in the living room of the farmhouse. I thought something was wrong. I really didn't know what until you told Brandy that you hoped I didn't know about the robbery or stolen car. When I stopped you for speeding yesterday, a routine check was made on your car tags.

When the name on your driver's license and the car registration didn't match, my captain called the State of Kentucky. This morning when I radioed him, I learned you were wanted for grand theft auto and bank robbery. Now, I'm a witness to your confession of those crimes. As for the counterfeit bills, you will need to take that issue up with your lawyer when you get one."

"What about my kids? What's going to happen to them?" Sims asked. He hoped the children would give him a way out of the arrest.

Chad shook his head. "You didn't think about them until it's to your benefit. I can assure you, we will take care of them. They will be placed with people who love and care for them. Now, get in the back of the car!" The Sargent had had enough of this guy. He helped Sims into the prisoner cage in the back seat of the car, locked the doors on both sides, and walked into the house.

***

The women were relieved to see Sargent Brown put George Sims in the cage in the back of the squad car. He secured the car doors so his prisoner wouldn't escape. Apparently, Sims had been arrested. They didn't know the charges. It didn't matter, he was gone. They were thankful to have him out of the house.

Once the women got past their relief it dawned on them, they would have to tell Brandy and Rick about their father's arrest. They weren't looking forward to that experience."

***

"Jay, I'm arresting this fellow. I will be back out in about an hour or so to get the Fairfield family. Their car isn't drivable as far as I can tell. You have your hands full freeing the rest of these cars." Chad yelled from across the driveway.

"Thank you, Chad. We still have a long way to go to have everyone out. What about his children?"

Chad had forgotten about them. "Keep them here. They can't go anywhere with anyone. They are in the custody of the State of Kentucky. I will have to take them to Protective Services in Chadron after I tend to the Fairfield family. As late as it is, I may have to do it tomorrow. Is it alright if they spend the night with you?"

"Sure, no problem. Annette won't mind the company for one more night. See you later, Chad!" Jay replied as he returned to his work.

***

When Bill Colton came into the house to take a break from the hard physical labor of snow removal, Mary pulls him aside into the laundry room. Closing the door behind her for a private talk. Bill suspected he knew what was coming. His wife probably wanted to discuss the Sims children. Mary had a real heart for children of any age.

"Was George Sims arrested?" Mary asked knowing the answer to her question.

"Yes. I don't know the charges. Chad Brown said he would explain later. All I know if that Sims is wanted in the State of Kentucky. Those children are wards of the State. They will have to be returned to Kentucky. I imagine Chad will send someone from Protective Services out here to get them." Bill knew the procedure. Bill and Mary had been state approved foster parents. The couple had had many children come stay with them at the farm over the years. Children who needed parental love.

"Bill, we can't let those precious children go to another foster home when we could care for them." Mary pleaded. "We are still state approved."

Bill couldn't argue with her. She loved children and was always their advocate. "Are you sure you can handle this? It tends to weigh on you physically and mentally. You get so attached to the children. Giving them up when they have to leave is so hard for you emotionally. I don't want you to wear yourself out trying to care for them and me."

"I won't. These are older children. They can help with the chores." Mary insisted.

"Yes, and one is an inexperienced teen parent. She will need extra help and training to caring for her son. Rick will need care and love as much as the other two. I think he's a very angry young man who hasn't been able to release that energy." Bill was exasperated. His speech was flying into the wind. Mary had already moved on with her own plans for the children. "You will have to call, Mrs. Blankenship, the social work supervisor in Lincoln to set this up. It would take a few days. What about seeing your mother? We will have to get permission to take the children into South Dakota, you know."

"Ok, dear. We can work it all out, I'm sure. I'll borrow Annette's telephone and give Mother a call. She will understand." That was true. Irene was just as big an advocate for children as Mary.

Bill smiled and walked into the kitchen for some hot coffee. The truth was, he enjoyed having children around their farm. They both loved kids. He just didn't want to upset Irene, his mother-in-law, by not coming to visit. He would have to rearrange in their Plymouth Fury to get the children in the car along with the rest of the things Mary brought for her mother. The little car was pretty full. Bill smiled to himself. He guessed they would be a little cozy on the way to Irene's house if they were allowed to take the children with them.

***

Henry Hapfield appeared in the house with his coat still on. He was cold and tired from removing snow from around the cars. They had just cleared the snow away from his car. Jay and the college students were working to get the Sims car out of the snow. That car would have to be moved so Henry could get out of the driveway and onto the highway. Henry's hands were stiff from the cold. His back ached. This office worker wasn't physically prepared for snow removal. Most of all, he needed a break. He could take a few minutes before going back outside. A cup of hot coffee would go a long way right now.

When Henry came in the front door, he saw Annette in the living room. "What do I owe you for the night's lodging and meals, Annette? You have really taken good care of me."

"Not a thing, Mr. Hapfield. We were glad we could help." Annette replied with a smile.

"Nonsense, take this," As he handed Annette a couple of twenty dollar bills rolled together. "This will help you kids out. If nothing else, use it for your son."

"No, we really don't need it. You may need this money when you get to Denver. It's perfectly fine. We hope your trip is safe and everything is alright with your father-in-law." Annette replied.

With Annette's back turned, Henry placed the bills on the top shelf of her curio cabinet. Henry hoped she would find the money when she cleaned house. His mission was accomplished. Bill noticed the action giving Henry a wink as an affirmative approval. When no one was looking, Bill did he same thing. He wanted to get back to work after Mary cornered him.

***

Bill and Henry had no more than finished their coffee when the college students returned to the kitchen table to warm themselves. The boys were very excited and talking at once.

"I can't believe it," Norman exclaimed. "I found the bottle right beside my car door in the snow. The bottle wasn't broken. The Schnapps is just chilled." Bill remembered seeing George Sims walking around David's car just before he was arrested. He must have been looking for that bottle to satisfy his cravings. It's miracle he didn't find it.

The boys continued their joking and kidding about Norman's miraculous find. They looked up only to see Professor Fairfield standing in the doorway of the kitchen with a frown on his face. He just woke up from a nap leaving Louise and the children sound asleep in the cozy bed. The boys didn't want the professor to find out about their alcohol which could get them expelled from school. A sinking feeling entered their stomachs when they realized they had just been caught breaking school rules for second time in two days. Skipping class was one thing, but this was far more serious.

"What do you have there, boys?" Dennis Fairfield asked as he sat down at the kitchen table. "Did you find something?"

"Well, Sir," Norman stubbled over his words, "I found a bottle of Peppermint Schnapps chilling in the snow."

"Imagine that! Where do you think it came from?"

"Well, Professor," Jason jumped to Norman's defense. "It's like this…"

"You might as well tell me the truth in front of these witnesses. I will find out one way or the other." Dennis said sternly. He was enjoying watching the boys' discomfort. They needed to learn a lesson. "It will go far better for you!"

"Ok, Sir, it's like this," David stated. He respected this tall broad shouldered history professor for his directness, openness, and honesty. "We decided to go to a concert in Denver as a break from studying. The concert is tonight." Looking at this wristwatch, David realized they wouldn't make it to Denver in time for the concert. "I don't think we will make it, though. Anyway, on the way out of town, I stopped at Donald's Drive Inn for food. Someone else in the car," David looked over at Jason. "decided to go over to the liquor store to purchase beer and the Schnapps."

"I'm over 21," Jason piped up in his own defense. "We didn't drink and drive. We drank it last night after we got to the Mills Farmhouse. As it turned out, we fell asleep after one beer each. Mr. Sims drank the rest and left the cans for us to clean up this morning. I was surprised when I saw Officer Brown sleeping in the recliner around the empty cans. Mr. Sims was asleep in that chair when I went to sleep. Funny thing, only part of the case was beside the chair! I suspect, Mr. Sims took the rest of the case into his bedroom to drink later."

"I see!" stated the professor. "There will be consequences for your actions because you purchased alcohol for a minor. Norman, if I remember correctly, you aren't of legal drinking age yet, are you? The dean and I will have to have a discussion about this when I return to the college campus."

Norman looked over at Jason. With a vehement tone to his voice, Norman stated, "I told you when you bought that stuff that it would be trouble!"

"Thank you, Mr. Lee for your honesty. Norman, you mean to tell me that you didn't request the alcohol in the first place. Why were you so excited when you found the Peppermint Schnapps?" Dr. Fairfield asked. He didn't understand the mixed signals Norman had given.

"Because sir, I didn't think we would find it. Like an idiot, I wasn't thinking when I walked into the house announcing my find. I guess I got wrapped up in the idea that the bottle was missing. I didn't think about the implications of its contents. I really don't care about drinking it. I just wanted to find the bottle." Norman kept taking deep breaths between his words. His panic showing with every word. "Jason didn't buy the beer and Schnapps for me. To look grown up, I drank part of one can of the beer. I dumped the rest in the bathroom sink before I went to bed. I really didn't care for the taste. I guess I was just going along for the ride."

"Just give me the bottle, Norman. Is there anything else anyone wants to add to Norman's statement." The professor asked. He could see the boys didn't have any ill intent. They just thought some alcohol would make them look more grown up.

"Only this sir, they argued about the purchase of the alcohol from Donald's Liquor to the state park," David added. "I was very unhappy with both of them. Just because, we are buddies doesn't mean we always agree! Norman thought the beer would get us in trouble. As it turned out, he was correct."

"Let me talk to the Dean of Students to see what he has to say. I will get back to you. Chances are you will get your bottle back, but I can't promise anything." Dennis felt sorry for the boys. They were trying so hard to be adults. What they didn't realize was that their actions spoke louder than their words. The students really will be good men someday. They just needed to mature. This is one of those experiences that will aid in their maturity.

***

Jay Mills came into the house stomping his feet in the doorway to release the snow from his boots and pant legs. "I was able to move the Sims car so you can get out of the driveway, Mr. Hapfield. As it turned out Sims left the keys in his car before he left with Officer Brown. The beast is out of everyone's way. It can stay parked at the edge of the driveway until someone comes and gets it. Stay as long as you like, but I know you are anxious to get to Denver to your wife and father-in-law." Jay explained. He was happy to help the man who had been such pleasant company. "I understand from the snow-plow crew, that the roads south to Alliance are basically clear. Just watch for slick spots after dark when the roads refreeze. Since Northwest Nebraska got the brunt of this storm, you should be able to reach Sydney without a problem."

"Thank you so much, Jay. You and Annette have been so good to me. I will never forget your hospitality. You are correct, I want to try to get to Denver tonight." Henry exclaimed putting his coat back over his shoulders.

"Did you remember everything you had with you? Do you need any snacks?" Annette asked. "Here's a sandwich that will hold you until you decide to stop along the way."

Henry smiled. The couple had really taken very good care of their unexpected company. Henry would miss his new friends in the farmhouse. He thought he had met some really good people in an unexpected way.

In a matter of minutes, Henry was driving to Alliance. He was so anxious to see Joan, he didn't think to call her. Then again, he had told her that he wouldn't call unless there was a problem. The snowplows had done an amazing job at clearing the roads. Snow was pushed into the ditches on both sides of the roads. Henry could only see black asphalt in front of him. The sun had come out adding a brightness to the snow. Henry located his sunglasses to remove the glare from the highway.

***

"Now that the Sims car has been moved, I think I can get my car out of the driveway too." David announced. "We aren't going to make it to the concert in Denver, which is starting in about an hour." David looked into the professor's eyes, knowing the responsible thing to do. "We had better get back to the dorm. I think we have had our break from studying. I know I have work to do."

"David, I know you have been having some problems in my class. Come by my office on Monday. We will see if we can help you pass." Dennis Fairfield offered. "History isn't easy for everyone! I understand, because science isn't easy for me."

"Thank you, Sir," David sighed with relief. "I will do that. Jason and Norman, are you ready to go? Do you have your sleeping bags rolled up? How about your extra clothing?"

"Yes, mother," Jason said sarcastically. "I'm ready to go and so is my little brother here." Pointing to Norman. Everyone laughed at the antics of the boys.

Within minutes they were heading down the road to Chadron. As they got to the Job Corps, Norman thought of something. "We didn't pay that nice couple for the food and shelter they provided us during the storm."

"Yes, we did. I added to the stack on money on the curio cabinet that someone else had started." David said with the pride of a man who had done something thoughtful for someone else.

***

Susan wondered into the bedroom to watch Brandy change Ethan's diaper. The baby had just awakened from his nap. At first, Brandy didn't quite know what to think of the caramel colored girl with bright shiny eyes. Susan's smiles light up her entire face. Brandy couldn't help but like her.

"Mark and I were thinking about going outside for a snowball fight. Would you and your brother like to join us?" Susan asked. She noticed the attention Brandy gave the baby. "How old are you anyway? Is this your baby?"

"I'm 15, yes, Ethan is my son," Brandy stated as she looked down at her son's diaper.

"That's the same age as me! I couldn't imagine having a baby right now. It must be really hard." Susan declared. She was so innocent. Her mother told her about teen parenthood, but she had never met a teen parent before.

"Sometimes it is really hard. I can't always do the things I want to do at times because Ethan's needs come first." Brandy voice was very sad. She had been through far more than Susan could ever imagine.

***

Bill and Mary Colton were standing in the doorway to the extra bedroom listening to the conversation between the girls. Their hearts went out to Brandy. She was only a child trying to raise another child. Bill wrapped a protective arm around his wife. He understood what she was feeling. Right now, he could punch

George Sims in the mouth for what he had done to his daughter. Bill pushed down his anger knowing it wouldn't change the present situation.

"Susan, can we have a word with Brandy and Rick before you go out to play in the snow. I haven't checked on your mother for a while. Please see if she needs anything." Mary instructed. She hoped Louise was still sleeping. It was the best medicine for her right now.

"I would be glad to, Mrs. Colton." Susan said as she walked out of the room. "The offer still stands when you are ready, Brandy. It will be fun to play in the snow before dark."

Brandy folded Rick into her arms with Ethan on her lap. She had learned when adults wanted to talk to them, it wasn't going to be good news. She hadn't seen her father for a couple of hours. Brandy thought he was still out shoveling snow. The teen couldn't imagine him working that hard though.

Chapter 12

A New Home

C+)

B ill and Mary pulled two wooden chairs put in front of the children so they could meet them eye to eye.

"We have some things to tell you, well more like to ask you," Bill said with a loving smile.

"How would you feel about coming to live with us at our farm in Beatrice?" An excited Mary piped in.

The children looked totally confused. How could this be happening?

"It's like this kids. You father was arrested by Officer Brown about an hour ago. I don't know the charges yet. You will need a place to stay until you go back to Kentucky. We have a state approved foster home in Beatrice. We thought we would get approval to take you with us. First, we wanted to make sure you wanted to go," Bill explained trying to sell the children on the couple's plans for them.

"I know why Dad was arrested. He shouldn't have taken that car or robbed the bank in Frankfurt last week." Thirteen year old Rick stated with the anguish of a boy who had seen an adult do some very foolish things. "I thought he would have been arrested before now. I was scared to death when Officer Brown stopped us for a speeding ticket before the snowstorm got so bad."

"I was really scared when I saw Officer Brown asleep on the recliner outside of this door. I was afraid he was guarding Dad. I was even more afraid the officer was going to take Ethan from me." Brandy admitted, her voice still shaking.

Bill and Mary were appalled. Over the years, they had heard some shocking stories, but this was one of the most egregious. George Sims was a real piece of work. He will be locked away for many, many years. Bill knew they would find out more about Sims' crimes when Officer Brown returned to the farm.

"We really want you to come live with us. There are lots of things to do on the farm. We have space enough in the house for each of you. You can have your own rooms including Ethan.

Brandy, I would be happy to help you care for Ethan so you can go to school. Your school is just down the road." Mary coaxed.

"I don't want to go back to Frankfurt! They were going to take Ethan from me." Brandy stated. She wasn't going to give up her son for anything. Looking at Rick, she said, "I think we should go with the Colton's. They are much nicer people than our last foster parents. What do you think, Ricky?"

"I'll give it a try," Rick declared. He was willing to go along with his sister. The idea of living on a farm sounded like an adventure. Rick didn't want to pass up some fun for a change.

"Very good!" Mary smiled. "I will try and get in touch with a friend of mine in Lincoln to get it arranged." She gave a loving touch to Brandy's extended leg. Mary walked out of the room with a mission in mind. Now to get past the party line ladies to make her telephone call before the Protective Services office closed.

***

"Does everyone have a heavy coat to play in the snow. That wind is very cold. You will need gloves for a snow-ball fight." Annette asked as she pulled extra coats from the living room closet. "I have put some extra coats and gloves on the couch. Take what you need. I don't want any more cases of frostbite."

Mary passed Annette standing in front of the closet. "Is it ok if I use your telephone? Bill and I will reimburse you for any long distance charges. I need to call a friend in Lincoln before 5:00." Annette could hear the urgency in Mary's voice. She was determined to help those children.

"Sure, no problem. We will deal with possible long distance charges later. We just need to get those kids taken care." Annette had a pretty good idea who Mary was going to call in Lincoln. They would do anything to help Brandy, Rick, and Ethan.

***

To Mary's surprise the telephone line wasn't in use when she picked up the receiver to make her call. A buzz could be heard on the other end of the line as the telephone rang into the Protective Services office.

"Good afternoon, this is Amanda Clayton. How may I direct your call?"

"Amanda, this is Mary Colton. Can I speak with Nancy Blankenship please? It's very important!"

"Mrs. Colton, yes. Mrs. Blankenship is available. I will transfer your call." Thank God, Mary thought. She was afraid reaching Nancy would be difficult. As the Protective Services Supervisor for Gage County, she was a very busy women.

"Hello, this is Nancy Blankenship. May I help you!"

"Nancy, this is Mary Colton. I need your help!"

"What's up? Mary, I haven't heard from you in months. Do you want to foster some additional children? We could sure use your help!" Nancy had worked with Mary Colton for years. She and her husband, Bill, loved children. When they fostered, they were all in which could really wear on them physically and emotionally.

"Let me explain. We are headed up to Hot Springs, South Dakota to visit my mother. She is running out of meat and vegetables. We decided to go for a visit before

Bill started spring planting. When we got up here to Chadron, we were caught in a sudden snowstorm. Due to an overturned tractor trailer on Highway 385, we couldn't go on into Chadron. We were directed to a farmhouse by the State Patrol to spend the night. The car is still loaded with the food for mother. We haven't been able to get to her yet. In the farmhouse we met a family from Kentucky…a father, teen parent, and a boy. The father was arrested today by the Nebraska State Patrol for crimes committed in Kentucky. The children are wards of the State of Kentucky, but they don't want to go back there. Frankly by their appearance, they weren't getting very good care in the previous foster home. The father brought them to Nebraska from Kentucky in a stolen car. The boy said his father robbed a bank on the way out of town with them in the car. This is a real messy case. There is more to tell, but too many people listening at the present time. Bill and I want to take custody of the children, take them with us to deliver the food stuffs to mother, and have them back in Beatrice no later than May 1." Mary tried to include all the details of the situation she could. "Would that be possible?"

"I have a couple of questions," Nancy stated. She always had questions. Nancy was one of those people who liked to have her ducks in a row before proceeding any further. "What are the name and ages of these children? Where is their mother? What county in Kentucky are they housed?"

Mary thought for a moment. "The children are Brandy Sims, age 15. Her son, Ethan Sims, age 4 months, her brother Rick Sims, age 13. It is my understanding that their mother is deceased. They were living in Frankfurt at the time they ran away to join their father on this trip."

"Do you have birth dates for these children?" Nancy asked.

"Just a moment, let me check." Mary stated. She knew there would be something she forgot to include. She spoke across the kitchen to the children. "Brandy, what is your date of birth?"

"September 9, 1962." Brandy replied.

"Do you know the dates of birth for Rick and Ethan?" Mary asked.

"Yes. Ethan's date of birth is December 15, 1976. Ricky's is March 13, 1964." Brandy replied. Proud of herself for being able to give some useful information.

"Did you get that Nancy?" Mary asked hoping to the end of the questions.

"Yes. I did. Let me check on this case. I don't know if Nebraska can take custody of the children from Kentucky without a court order or at the very least a temporary order. We will have to get permission from Kentucky to take them to South Dakota. It will help that you are Approved Nebraska Foster Parents." Nancy explained. Her mind wandering to the legal ramifications of the situation. "I need to call the Nebraska State Patrol. Kyle Jacobson will tell me what charges the father faces and if he will be in police custody for an indefinite period of time. Then I will try to reach Kentucky Protective Services to see if they are willing to cooperate with us. Since it's so late in the day, it maybe tomorrow before I hear back from them. Keep the children at the farmhouse with you. Don't allow them to go anywhere with anyone else. Can you hold off your trip to South Dakota for one more day?"

"I think so." Mary was disappointed, she wanted to see her mother. The snowstorm had already delayed them. With permission from the Mills, she gave their telephone number to Nancy. "I will talk to you tomorrow. Thank you, Nancy."

"You are welcome. These children are very fortunate to have you and Bill on their side. I'll call back just as soon as I get some word." Nancy didn't know if this would work out. Those children certainly needed her help.

***

After Mary placed the telephone receiver into its cradle, she turned to find Brandy standing right behind her holding Ethan. A look of fear covered her sweet face. Mary's heart went out to the child.

"Are they coming to take us away?" Brandy anxiously asked.

"No, darling, the three of you are to stay here with us for the night. Mrs. Blankenship has to make some telephone calls to Kentucky to get permission for you to come with us. The best thing for you to do is pray the Lord wants you to remain with Bill and I."

"Prayers don't work for me!" Brandy's crestfallen face told Mary that she didn't know about Jesus. That is another lesson Mary and Bill would teach to the children.

"Sweetheart, God has a plan for you. You'll see! It will all workout in His perfect timing." Mary was planting seeds for Brandy's future. Brandy just didn't know it yet. "I have an idea. Why don't you let me finish feeding Ethan? I would love to cuddle him for a little bit. We need to get acquainted. You can go out with the other children to play in the snow. Some exercise would do you good. Don't worry about Ethan, I will take good care of him while you are gone." Mary suggested. She really wanted the child outside. Mary didn't want the child to hear what she had to tell her husband and the other adults in the room.

"Are you sure about this?" Brandy asked. "He's a handful."

Mary smiled. "I've taken care of lots of children. Believe me, he will be just fine."

"You can borrow one of my extra winter coats over there on the couch," Annette stated in a cheery voice catching onto Mary's reasoning for having the child outside. "Let me get it for you!"

***

Just as Brandy started out the back door headed to the snowball fight; Sargent Brown pulled into the front yard. He was tired from several long days of work. Chad had much more to do before his shift ended. Going home was beginning to sound really good to him. He hadn't seen his family in the last forty eight hours.

"Come on in, Chad. Would you like some coffee and a chance to warm up?" Jay asked as he greeted the patrolman at the front door.

"Would I ever! How is everyone doing? What about Mrs. Fairfield?" Chad asked. He had been concerned about getting her to medical attention.

"My patient is resting comfortably. She has been asleep for a couple of hours which is the best medicine. With all the noise in the house, I'm surprised she has slept this long." Annette stated.

***

Dennis Fairfield heard the mention of his wife's name and came into the living room with Chad and Annette. "She was extremely exhausted from our trip to North Platte yesterday and sitting in the cold car for so many hours last night. I've checked on her several times. She seems to be fine. When I noticed your car Sargent Brown, I thought about waking her up."

"Let's allow her to sleep for a little longer. I need to talk to the Mills and Coltons. I'm glad the children are outside. Dr. Fairfield, you can join us if you like. I have some things to tell you." Chad stated with a grim look on his face.

"Come on in. I will pour the coffee. We have something to tell you too." Annette stated.

The patrolman sat down at the kitchen table and waited for everyone to join him. In a few minutes everyone was seated around the large table. Coffee cups full of freshly brewed coffee and freshly baked cookies available for dunking.

"These cookies look really good. Annette, did you make them?" Chad asked.

"No, I can't take credit for them. Mary brought them in her basket of goodies. That basket had some amazing things in it." Annette laughed as she looked over at her new friend. "I'm so thankful she brought them with her."

"You are very welcome." Mary was pleased at the complement.

***

With that statement, Chad began his story, "George Sims has been arrested and charged with bank robbery, grand theft auto, kidnapping, endangering the lives of three minors, and passing counterfeit bills in three states maybe more. It seems he had the children in the car with him when he robbed the bank in Frankfurt, Kentucky. The fast thinking bank teller gave him a bag of counterfeit money that they had used for a training exercises. Sims was in such a big hurry. He didn't even notice the quality of the bills. I'm not sure why he didn't notice when he made his purchases or why some clerk didn't notice. This guy will be in jail for a very long time!" Chad explained. "The car in your driveway is the stolen vehicle. I see it was moved. I made Sims leave the keys in it before I arrested him. I thought you would need to move that beast to get the other vehicles out of your driveway."

"I'm sure glad you thought to leave the keys. What do we do with the car? I don't like the idea of having stolen property in our yard for very long." Jay asked. "Will it be moved soon?"

"Tomorrow, I will bring another patrolman with me. We will take the car back to the Chadron impound yard until someone comes to get it from Kentucky. I hope we can have it returned to the rightful owners in a couple of weeks. We need to dust it for fingerprints, so no one get in the car. If the children need something from the car, let them. Their prints are all over the car anyway. Just take care not to add new ones. Jay we will take note that you drove the car to move it in your yard." Jay nodded in agreement.

***

Noticing the officer's coffee cup was almost empty, Dennis Fairfield got up from the table. He really didn't want to hear any additional information about the Sims family. It was really too much to take in. "I think

I will go wake up, Louise. She will need some time to assemble herself before traveling back to Chadron." Dennis placed his coffee cup in the kitchen sink. He wanted to give Louise time to awaken and dress herself. He walked out of the kitchen toward the larger of the two bedrooms.

"Chad, there is a couple of things you need to know. First of all, Bill and I will take custody of the children. We have contacted Protective Services in Lincoln. We are an approved foster home. It seems the children are in the custody of the State of Kentucky. The Gage County supervisor is working on the logistics of transferring them from Kentucky to Nebraska. One other thing, your Captain needs to be aware. From Brandy's own admission, George is Ethan's father." Mary Colton stated making the officer aware of the entire situation.

"You mean…" the startled look on Chad's face told it all. The captain had been correct!

"I'm afraid so." Replied Mary looking at the remainder of people in the room.

"We may be adding to Sim's charges. I will make the Captain aware, if he doesn't already know. He's been gathering information on this family all day. I probably should get going to Chadron. I've had a long few days and could use some sleep. I'm off duty for the next couple of days. Is Mrs. Fairfield ready to go?" It was apparent that Chad had had his fill for the day. This Sims case was too much!

"I will check," Annette stated. With her simple statement, Louise Fairfield walked slowly into the room.
"How are you doing, Mrs. Fairfield?"

"My feet free like they are on fire. I can't hardly walk!"
The pain was noticeable on her beautiful face.

"Mrs. Fairfield, I'm going to take you to Chadron.
The Medical Clinic has closed for the day, so we are
going to the Hospital emergency room." Chad explained.

"What about my family?" Louise whined. "How will
they get back to Chadron. We live there."

"Since your car isn't drivable and will need to be
towed out of the ditch, your husband and children can
ride with us." Chad Brown instructed.

"If it's alright with you officer, would you drop us
by our house instead of the hospital? We have an extra
car. I can leave the children at home to raid the refrigerator while I take Louise to the hospital. That way, you
wouldn't have to wait for us." Dennis suggested. This
officer had been really good to them. Dennis knew he
had to be exhausted. "I can make the arrangements to
have the Blazer towed after Louise is attended to."

Chad was relieved at the plan. He really wanted to
get home to his recliner. "That sounds like a good idea
to me! Are your kids ready to go? I almost forgot to tell
you, Professor, Wahlstrom Ford is sending a tow truck
to get your Blazer either this evening or in the morning.
When they called me last night to go find you, they
stated they would come after your car after the storm

ended. I would call them when you get home to make the needed arrangements for payment, etc."

***

Right on cure, the three of the four teens walked to the house. Stomping the snow from their feet and removing the gloves from their hands. The children had broad smiles on their faces. They were cold, but happy. Their bodies were still covered with the telltale signs of the crystalized liquid. Twelve year old Mark came running into the farmhouse behind them with excitement in his voice, "Do you know what we saw? Baby lambs playing in the barn yard. They were running in and out of the barn playing like children. Dad, they are so cute! Want to come outside and see them?"

"Some other time son. We need to get your mother into the doctor as soon as we can. Maybe we can come back out to the farm to visit another day." Dennis stated hoping for an educational day for his children. He wouldn't mind another visit with the Mills family when things calmed down for both families.

"You would be welcome anytime. If you come when the ground is dry, we can saddle the horses and go for a ride." Jay offered.

"Can we Dad?" Susan asked. The horses had far more appeal to her than the baby lambs.

"We'll see." Dennis told his children. He wasn't sure they would visit the farm again, but he hoped so.

Dennis's eye contact with his children told them he was ready to leave. "We are riding to Chadron with Sargent Brown. He will drop us off at home while I take your mother to see a doctor at the Hospital." Dennis instructed. "Jay and Annette, thank you for your hospitality and loving care. You are really special people. Bill and Mary, it has been a pleasure to meet you. Thank you all for everything. Hope to see each of you again. Let's go gang!"

Dennis and Officer Brown led Louise to the front seat of the patrol car. Annette was glad she had thought to cover Louise's feet the rags to keep them warmer in the snow since Louise didn't have any warm shoes or socks. They are very nice people, Annette thought. I hope we see them again.

***

The living room cleared out quickly. The remaining wet clothing was removed from the front doorway to the laundry room where Annette would wash and dry each article. "How about some hot chocolate?" Annette asked Brandy and Rick. "It will taste really good after being in the cold air! I'll bet you could use a cookie or two. I imagine you are starving."

"I sure am." Rick replied. Annette noticed the boy was coming out his shell after he knew his father was gone.

"How is Ethan, is he alright?" Brandy asked. Sounding very much like a worried mother.

"Come in the kitchen and see." Annette instructed. "Mary has been taking very good care of him." The infant was sitting on Mary's lap with smiles over his cubby face. He was getting all kinds of attention from Bill. "I think I heard Seth. He's probably ready for a change and his supper. I usually feed him before Jay, and I eat our supper. It's quieter that way!" Everyone chuckled. They all knew Seth took food seriously.

"Annette, you and Jay wouldn't happen to have some extra clothing that would fit Brandy and Rick, would you?" Mary asked. "I thought it would be a good idea to have them take a bath. I'm sure they would enjoy feeling fresh and clean."

"Yes. I think I can find some jeans and T-shirts that will fit them. I was going to give Seth a bath after his supper. We can include Ethan in that process, so everyone feels fresh and clean tonight." Annette replied.

Annette's cheerfulness over a simple thing like a bath disturbed Rick. "A bath!!! I have to take a bath!!!" he exclaimed. "No, I won't!"

Bill chuckled. "Women just have to have everything clean. That's one of Life's Storms, my boy! Just go along for the ride."

Epilogue

Three Years Later…

～✦～

A nnette Mills walked outside to their mailbox in Rapid City, South Dakota. She was thrilled to see a letter from Mary Colton. Annette's mind wandered back to the snowy day in April when she first met Mary and her husband, Bill. Annette's husband, Jay, brought them into their little farmhouse in Chadron, Nebraska. Mary was prepared for any emergency. Annette was very thankful for Mary and Bill's help during their isolation. Annette and Jay's son, Seth, was a newborn. Annette needed the extra pair of hands to care for 14 extra people. The Nebraska Highway Patrol brought them to their home during a sudden snowstorm. What a group they were!

Annette and Jay no longer resided on the farm which belonged to his grandfather. After Granddad passed away, his children decided to sell the property on the Table. Jay was able to follow his dream of becoming a mining engineer. He is attending the South Dakota School of Mines in Rapid City. Annette has been working as a nurse at the Veteran's Hospital in Hot Springs. Little Jennifer joined the family a year ago giving Seth a playmate.

Annette sat down to read Mary's monthly letter. Bill is thinking about retiring but isn't sure he wants to make that step. The adoption of Brandy, Rick, and Ethan was finalized two years ago when their father gave up his parental rights. Brandy wants to attend the University of Nebraska next fall. Both Brandy and Rick are doing very well in school. Ethan has become another grandchild to Bill and Mary. George Sims was convicted on all counts. He was sentenced to 40 years without parole. The children never asked about him or to see him.

A week or so after everyone left Jay and Annette's farmhouse, she found $80.00 in cash on their curio cabinet. They did as Henry Hapfield suggested. The funds were put into a savings account for Seth. About two weeks after Henry left the house when the roads were cleared, he sent a photo album for Seth's baby pictures. Inside the photo album was a note that stated his father-in-law, Paul passed away the night after Henry stayed at the farmhouse. Annette hasn't heard from Henry since that last note.

The tow truck from Wahlstrom's Ford pulled the Blazer belonging to the Fairfield family out of the ravine. After the snow melted, Jay and Annette went out to visit the site of the accident. If the car had landed five feet either direction, it would have been impossible to get the passengers out of the car because the Blazer would have been too deeply wedged into the ravine below. It was a miracle the family wasn't killed on impact. Only the pillow of snow and the Lord saved them. Dennis Fairfield is still teaching history at Chadron State College. Dennis has become involved in various historical organizations around the Chadron area. Louise is a beloved teacher in the elementary schools. Susan will graduate Chadron High School this spring. Mark will move from Chadron Middle School to Chadron High School next fall. He wants to play football for the Chadron Cardinals in his freshman year. The family has become a vital part of the culture of Northwest Nebraska.

David Abram passed his history class with Dr. Fairfield. He transferred to the University of Nebraska Medical School. He is currently working very hard to become Dr. Abrams. Jason Lee graduated from Chadron State College with an accounting degree last fall. The last Annette heard he was working in an accounting firm in Scottsbluff. Norman Gray graduated with a teaching certificate. He was hired to teach math at the Valentine High School. He was thrilled to be working in his hometown where he could take care of his elderly parents.

The last Annette and Jay had heard from Officer Chad Brown was when they sold Jay's grandfather's farm. Most of the contents of the farm had been auctioned off. Officer Brown provided traffic control on and off of Highway 385 during the auction.

A total of 14 people were rescued from the freezing temperatures, high winds, and blowing snow on that

April 1977 day. Officially the depths of the snow were announced to be twenty four inches. The winds piled the snow into drifts that reached the top of the hay loft on Jay's barn. It took weeks for the Nebraska sun to melt the unexpected spring snow.

Thank God, no one was injured or killed. Praise Him for his Goodness and Mercy!

Author's Notes

This is a true story. The Blizzard in mid-April 1977 happened. I was a witness. I lived in the farmhouse when the Nebraska State Patrol called to ask for assistance. Our oldest son was 2 months old. We gathered anything we could find to wrap people up to keep them warm in the drafty little house with only a gas stove to warm them. We weren't blessed to have cots for everyone to sleep on. Only the cold floor, sleeping bags, air mattresses, a sectional couch, and one bed kept everyone warm. Several of the men simply slept in their clothing on the floor. Our residence was a farmhouse that truly was the last house on the highway 15 miles south of Chadron. From that house, there isn't another farm on the highway until you reach Hemingford even today.

A cold front followed the jet stream bringing with it extremely cold temperatures. The temperatures that night dropped to negative 2 degrees. High winds blew the drifting snow everywhere. Visibility on the highway was zero. The state patrol established a roadblock in front of our house. No one was allowed to travel south to Alliance nor were they allowed to travel north to Chadron. Road conditions were too severe. There wasn't an internet to give people the latest road reports on the Weather Channel. There was only one television station, one radio station, and the telephone with a party line. In 1977, the road from Chadron to Alliance was a 60 mile stretch with no restaurants, no motels, or convenience stores. Certainly, no cell phone service. Neighbors helping neighbors is a way of life on the Plains. It becomes necessary for everyone's survival.

Even today, once you leave either city, there aren't very many places to stop and rest. Keeping extra blankets, pillows, coats, and snacks is a necessity in the winter months in the event of a sudden storm. People who live in the area make sure the gasoline tanks in their cars never get below a quarter of a tank. If they end up in a snow drift, they want to have enough fuel to keep them warm. Additional cell towers have been placed in the area to make cell services better but there are still a few areas in the Sandhills where cell service is questionable.

Some poetic license was taken with this story. For instance...The tractor trailer accident was fictional. The human compositions of the vehicles were correct, but the passengers' names and background stories are out of my imagination. The truth is, for the most part, we didn't get to know our houseguests all that well before they were back on the roads again. The incident with the money on the curio cabinet was true as was the photo album sent to my son. The incident with the party lines was true, but the names were changed. It was many years before I knew the luxury a private telephone line. The three young college students staying as our guests did lose a quart bottle of Peppermint Schnapps in the snow on the way into our house. As in the story, the Schnapps was found beside the wheels of the car the next morning. It was well chilled and ready for consumption, but never brought into the house.

The businesses mentioned in this book were open and real in 1977. Most of them are closed now with a few exceptions. Wahlstrom's Ford still remains open. The Favorite Bar on Main Street in Chadron remains open. It is a main stay for Chadron's history and culture. Chuck Wagon was destroyed in a fire in 2005. Donald's Drive Inn (so named for its owner) changed management and was closed a few years ago. Forever lost in Nebraska's rich history are the one room schools of Highland Center and Table Center. Instead of students walking, riding horses, or riding on the fender of their father's tractors in deep snow, they are bused twenty miles from the Table to Hemingford. Chadron State College, Chadron East Ward School, Chadron Middle School, and Chadron High School are still open. Chadron State Park, the Fur Trade Museum, and Fort Robinson near Crawford are wonderful places to learn about the rich history of Northwest Nebraska. Feel free to visit my hometown! There is lots to see and do.

Special thanks to The Nebraska State Patrol who are still offering their services to the state. At times, they work in horrific weather conditions. To those patrolmen who were working on Highway 385 in 1977, you were marvelous. Thank you for your hard work and dedication to duty.

A special tribute to Jerry Dishong who devoted over 50 years of his life as a news anchor on KDUH-TV out of Scottsbluff. Often, he was the only source of news to hundreds of people. KLRC has served the citizens of Northwest Nebraska for years. They can now be heard on the internet on Chadrad.com.

Special thanks to the people who helped with this book. My proofreaders and editors have been marvelous. God Bless you!

For God so loved the world,
that he gave his only Son,
that whoever believes in him (Jesus)
should not perish but have eternal life.
John 3:16 ESV

CPSIA information can be obtained
at www.ICGtesting.com
Printed in the USA
LVHW030221210522
719348LV00001B/1